Thomas Lillie is an experienced solicitor specialising in financial services disputes. His practice includes advising secured lenders, receivers and other creditors on a range of contentious issues, with a particular focus on receivership and litigation arising out of secured lending.

A Practical Guide to Property Receivership

A Practical Guide to Property Receivership

Thomas Lillie, solicitor

Law Brief Publishing

Published 2026 by Law Brief Publishing, an imprint of Law Brief Publishing Ltd
30 The Parks
Minehead
Somerset
TA24 8BT

www.lawbriefpublishing.com

Paperback: 978-1-918241-19-8

For I.L.

PREFACE

Introduction

This work concerns the appointment of fixed charge or Law of Property Act receivers over property in England & Wales by mortgage lenders.

Receivership in the mortgage context is a remedy available to mortgage lenders. Fundamentally, it offers mortgage lenders a powerful tool in which to secure repayment of the money owed to it when a borrower has defaulted. It is a tripartite relationship between the lender, the borrower and the receivers, created by the mortgage which grants the receivers some quite unique powers and subjects them to some onerous duties.

Receivership allows lenders to appoint a third party to, in effect, take control of the secured property, manage it, and recover income or sale proceeds to pay down the debt owed to the lender. The lender stands at arm's length, removed from the day-to-day challenges of managing the property, which is entrusted to the receivers. To a significant degree the appointment of receivers insulates the lender from liability and in more complex cases it enables a considered exit strategy to be devised; effectively imposing a new management team upon complex developments or portfolios.

Although it is a well-established concept, there is no clear or encompassing explanation of receivership either in statute or case law. Indeed, there is a relatively little case law or regulation when compared to other areas of property or financial services law. The key statutory instrument remains the Law of Property Act 1925. The statutory provisions in the Law of Property Act 1925 are very limited, and for this reason, the powers of receivers are usually significantly extended by contractual provisions within the mortgage agreement.

Despite the dearth of statutory provisions, case law or regulation, receivership is nevertheless, an increasingly well-used remedy, but there remains a lack of understanding of the role, duties and powers of receivers and their appointing lenders.

Aim

This text is intended to offer a brief and practical guide for busy practitioners. It is suited to experienced practitioners seeking a short reference guide, as well as those who may be new to the area or who perhaps encounter it infrequently.

An aim of this work is to also provide some practical and legal guidance for each party to the tripartite relationship. This is with the intention of enhancing knowledge and familiarity with the concepts and the duties and powers of receivers, thereby reducing friction and ill-founded challenges so efforts can focus on achieving positive outcomes.

This text is not an exhaustive analysis of the law and intentionally avoids commenting on areas of academic or jurisprudential debate, of which there are several pertaining to receivership. There are some references to key pieces of legislation, official guidance and useful case law but again, such references are not intended to be exhaustive. Some topics warrant a closer look at case law authorities and some quotations are used where this helps to illustrate the point.

Receivership touches many other areas of general or specialist law which are outside of the scope of this work. The focus of this work is receivership in the mortgage context, being fixed charge receivership, and receivership under the Law of Property Act 1925. With regard to the secured asset, the text focusses on real property, as opposed to other secured assets. It covers the full life cycle of a receivership, from pre-appointment considerations, appointment, receiver powers and duties, through to sale of the secured property, litigation, challenges and termination of the receivership.

Outside the scope of this text are more specialist areas of receivership, such as court appointed receivers under Part 69 of the Civil Procedure Rules 1998, agricultural receivers or administrative receivers.

In relation to terminology, this text refers to a mortgagee as a lender or secured lender and to mortgagors as borrowers. The term receivers is usually used in the plural reflecting the common practice of appointing two individuals to be joint receivers.

The law is stated as 31 January 2026. Any mistakes are my own.

Thomas Lillie
January 2026

CONTENTS

CHAPTER ONE

PRE-APPOINTMENT

1. Introduction

1.1. The appointment of receivers is one of several enforcement methods that a secured lender will consider when faced with a borrower in default. Some lenders will have a clearly defined process as to which enforcement method they will use and what steps they will take given a particular set of circumstances. Receivers will often be appointed when the secured property is either a commercial, mixed use or residential "buy-to-let" investment property. Receivers are not commonly appointed where the borrower is in occupation of the secured property.

1.2. This chapter provides guidance on steps a lender and their advisers may take prior to the appointment of receivers. Some of those steps are optional but may be recommended depending on the circumstances. Other steps are mandatory if a receiver appointment is to be validly made.

Security Review

1.3. A security review is a document prepared for a lender containing advice as to the enforceability of the security held in the lender's favour. Its purpose is to advise the lender on practical or theoretical risks it may face concerning the mortgage documentation and enforceability, if it decides to enforce its security or exercise its remedies.

1.4. Lenders may require a security review as part of their decision making on whether to appoint receivers or other pursue other remedies. The security review may be commissioned after the lender has identified a breach of covenant or event of default on the borrower's part, or it may be commissioned in anticipation of a breach. It may be commissioned alongside other sources of information concerning the borrower's financial position.

1.5. Many lenders have specific requirements as to what a security review should investigate and report upon and the circumstances in which a security review is required. Practitioners should ascertain whether the lender has any such processes or policies to ensure they are followed, and whether the lender has a particular form of security review that it requires.

1.6. Absent any specific requirements, a security review would ordinarily involve: collating documentation and information from the lender, undertaking external searches to obtain further information, analysing the information obtained and preparing a written report.

Security documents and other information from the lender

1.7. It will be necessary to obtain all contractual security and ancillary documents from the lender. The documentation concerning a standard residential buy-to-let mortgage may consist of only a mortgage offer, legal charge and mortgage terms and conditions. However, more complex lending arrangements may include: facility letters or loan offers, legal charges, debentures, all sets of terms and conditions incorporated into the aforementioned documents (noting that there may be several), collateral security documents, personal and corporate guarantees, board minutes, any intercreditor agreement or deed of priority. Ideally original documents or certified copies should be provided but it is not uncommon for the lender to simply have retained non-certified copies.

1.8. It may also be necessary to establish the corporate structure of the borrower, shareholders and directors in relation to a corporate borrower. The lender may be able to furnish this information which can be checked against Companies House records using the online public search facility.[1]

1.9. A lender may also provide any evidence it may have as to a potential default and should furnish other important information, such as the outstanding debt balance and any arrears, or other information concerning financial or non-financial breaches, along with any valuations of secured assets (historical and recent). All of this information will help to assess whether the borrower is in default and what enforcement options the lender may have, and, in the event of a possession claim, what the court may order.

Searches

1.10. It is necessary to conduct relevant searches to ascertain whether required forms of security are correctly registered and identify any other relevant entries on the public record. Searches should include: HM Land Registry and Companies House.

HM Land Registry

1.11. A proprietorship search should be conducted in relation to a corporate borrower in order to identify property owned by the company. Once a registered property is identified, an office search without priority should be conduced in order to obtain official copies of the register of title. It is critically important

---

1 see paragraph 1.16

to undertake a new HM Land Registry search, rather than rely on historical official copies of the register of title that date from the time of the lending because they will not record recent entries which may be adverse to the lender's position.

1.12. There are restrictions on searching HM Land Registry for properties owned by individuals, as detailed in Practice guide 74: searches of the index of proprietors' names.[2] Instead, official copies of the register of title for any relevant or secured properties known, or thought to be owned, solely or jointly by the individual borrower should be obtained.

1.13. Any documents referred to within official copies of the register of title and noted to be held by HM Land Registry should also be obtained. For example, copies of legal charges referred to within the charges register and copies of leases in relation to leasehold property.

1.14. An official search in respect of home rights to ascertain whether any third parties have a right to redeem the mortgage or remedy any breach (a home rights search may also later need to be produced in possession proceedings).

1.15. For individual borrowers or individual guarantors, a land charges bankruptcy search should be undertaken.[3]

Companies House

1.16. Online searches of Companies House public records should be conducted for all corporate borrowers and corporate

---

2 https://www.gov.uk/government/publications/searches-of-the-index-of-proprietors-names/practice-guide-74-searches-of-the-index-of-proprietors-names

3 https://www.gov.uk/guidance/land-registry-portal-how-to-make-a-bankruptcy-search

guarantors incorporated in England & Wales. Searches can be conducted using the company name or company registration number using the Companies House online search facility.[4]

1.17. All relevant documents should be obtained from Companies House. These may include: all outstanding registered charges and debentures, any notices of receiver appointment, company memorandum and articles of association, all filings concerning director appointments and resignations.

1.18. Pursuant to section 859K of the Companies Act 2006, notice of a receiver appointment is required to be given to the registrar of companies which is then recorded on the public search facility. It is important for a lender to understand whether other creditors have already appointed receivers in relation to a corporate borrower's assets.

Other

1.19. Depending on the nature of the lending facility and the requirements of the lender, further searches may be recommended, such as the trademark and patent register, Central Register of Winding Up Petitions by telephone[5] and an online search of the *London Gazette* for any insolvency notices.[6]

4 https://find-and-update.company-information.service.gov.uk/

5 Central Register of Winding Up Petitions telephone number: 0906 754 0043 and website: https://www.gov.uk/courts-tribunals/companies-list

6 https://www.thegazette.co.uk/

Analysis of Security Documents and Search Results

1.20. Once the documentation and search results have been obtained, it will be necessary to analyse the material. The following issues will need to be considered:

- Has security documentation been correctly executed?
- Has the legal mortgage been executed by deed in accordance with the formalities for an individual borrower[7] or corporate borrower[8] (as applicable)?
- Has security documentation been correctly registered at HM Land Registry in the case of real property and, in the case of a corporate borrower, Companies House?
- If security is not registered, or registered incorrectly, what effect does this have on the lender's rights?
- Does the security have priority over other secured creditors?
- Did a corporate borrower have the power to borrow and grant security over company assets?
- Are there records indicating that other creditors have taken legal action, such as other receiver appointments made in respect of a corporate borrower, winding up petitions or bankruptcy entries?
- Did the directors of a corporate borrower have authority?

---

7 Section 1 of the Law of Property (Miscellaneous Provisions) Act 1989

8 Sections 43 to 52 of the Companies Act 2006. There are difference requirements for Limited Liability Partnerships and other entities

- What contractual covenants or obligations have been breached (if any)?

- Has an event of default occurred which may trigger the option to exercise certain remedies?

- What formalities are contained in the documentation regarding enforcement? For example, is a formal demand required? Is the borrower entitled to notice and a period of time to remedy the breach? What are the service requirements and how would service be proved?

1.21. The security review should specify whether the lender has the power to appoint fixed charge receivers or Law of Property Act receivers[9] and what powers the receivers will enjoy. If there are any key deficiencies or omissions in those powers, then this should be highlighted in the security review, together with a summary of any other potential issues, risks or deficiencies with the security, its registration or the title of the secured property. If there are title issues, it may be prudent for the security review to recommend that the lender obtains a specialist report on title in relation to the secured property.

1.22. The security review should identify any risks or vulnerabilities as to the security and likely challenges. Similarly, any deficiencies in relation to the registration of the security at HM Land Registry and, in the case of corporate borrowers, at Companies House, should be highlighted, together with the effect these deficiencies may have on the lender's ability to enforce the security and exercise its remedies.

---

9 See paragraph 1.42 regarding fixed charge receivers vs Law of Property Act receivers

Enforcement Options

1.23. The security review should identify the lender's enforcement options, based on the documentation and search results analysed, and any other information provided by the lender.

1.24. If there is evidence to show that an event of default has occurred, or that the borrower or guarantor is in breach of any obligations, the lender will likely have a number of remedies and enforcement options available to them. These may include the right to appoint administrators or administrative receivers of a corporate borrower, the right to petition for the bankruptcy of an individual borrower or the right to appoint fixed charge receivers over assets of an individual or corporate borrower secured by a fixed charge.

1.25. Following receipt of the security review, a lender may be able to make a decision as to whether to proceed with the appointment of a receiver or whether other enforcement options are more desirable.

Receiver Pre-appointment report

1.26. In some cases, the lender may ask the proposed receiver to prepare a report on the prospective receivership. This may include the likely strategy to achieve redemption of the debt or other options and an indicative or "desktop" valuation of the secured asset.[10]

1.27. At this stage, the receiver should also have regard to the risks associated with the appointment. Examples such risks include: onerous property which may be damaged, contaminated or a

[10] A desktop valuation is one conducted from a desk, as opposed to a more detailed valuation conducting following a physical inspection

risk to third parties or public; high risk occupiers or use, for example, if the property is believed to be used for criminal purposes; insurance arrangements and costs, whether the receivers may require an indemnity from the lender[11] or whether there are wider commercial or reputational risks. Arrangements for the receivers' remuneration should also be considered.[12]

Default and Demand

Options for a Lender

1.28. The lender will usually have obtained advice on enforcement options in the form of a security review or otherwise. The lender's aim will often be to take proportionate action to recover the debt owed by the borrower, including any interest and costs, factoring in the costs of the various options considered below, whilst seeking to take into consideration the interests of the borrower, where possible. The appointment of a receiver is unlikely to be the only option available to a lender. Lenders would be well advised to consider the alternatives although the appointment of receivers is commonly a swift and cost-effective way in which to achieve redemption of the secured debt without taking direct action against the borrower.

1.29. The lender should give consideration to the wider circumstances, such as an assessment of the estimated value of the secured property at the present time, against the secured debt, to ascertain the estimated equity value (or loss) in the property, and whether certain actions, such as the appointment of receivers, may trigger cross-default provisions

11 See paragraph 2.72 regarding indemnities

12 See paragraph 2.76 regarding remuneration

in other facilities, either with that same lender or with others. Lenders may choose to work with prospective receivers, insolvency advisers, valuers and solicitors to obtain professional advice on these issues, particularly in complex or high value situations.

1.30. Options for a lender will commonly include negotiation, expressly reserving rights, insolvency or other legal action, or the appointment of receivers. We shall consider each in turn.

1.31. Negotiation with the borrower: When considering whether negotiation may be worthwhile, lenders should consider:

- Whether the default can be remedied in a reasonable period of time (and in the case of arrears, whether the borrower is likely to be able to pay off the sums by the end of the term)?[13]

- Whether the event of default or breach is significant or fundamental to the relationship or one creating material risks for the lender? Or whether it is something less significant, perhaps not causing a material risk to the lender or being technical in nature?

- Whether the borrower may be able to make arrangements to redeem the mortgage debt, such as by way of refinance (remortgaging with another lender), capitalising any arrears, offering the lender further security assets, or by making a single lump sum or a series of payments to reduce the debt balance and/or pay down any arrears?

---

13 See *Cheltenham and Gloucester Building Society v Norgan* [1996] 1 All ER 449 in relation to mortgage arrears where a reasonable period of time was considered, as a starting point, to be the remaining term of the mortgage

- Are there any extenuating circumstances which may justify the lender exercising forbearance?

1.32. Such negotiations are commercial in nature and the lender should have regard to any contractual rights, remedies or obligations contained in the security documentation as well as its own policies and procedure and any applicable regulatory obligations or codes of conduct.

1.33. Reservation of rights: Whilst negotiations are underway or otherwise where the lender requires some time to consider its options, lenders may elect to issue a "reservation of rights" letter. A reservation of rights letter is often issued by a lender and served on the borrower when a breach of the facility agreement or an event of default has occurred or is expected to occur, but before the lender has decided on whether to take formal enforcement action. It is intended to notify the borrower of the breach or event of default and reserve the lender's rights in relation to the specific breach or event, thereby preventing the borrower from later asserting that any delay in the lender taking action amounted to a waiver of its right to do so or otherwise amounting to an acquiescence of the breach. Often there is an express term in the mortgage that forbearance on the lender's part will not amount to the waiver of any rights.

1.34. Direct legal action: The lender may have an option to take direct legal action against the borrower, which may involve a claim for possession of the secured property and/or a money judgment. Consideration should also be given as to whether action is appropriate against any corporate or individual guarantors.

1.35. Insolvency action: The lender may have the right to petition for the bankruptcy of the borrower or any individual guarantor or appoint administrators or issue a winding up petition.

These actions have wide ranging consequences and will only be appropriate in certain circumstances. The lender should obtain professional advice from insolvency experts.

1.36. Appointment of a fixed charge or Law of Property Act receiver: The first step in assessing whether a receiver can be appointed is to consider the terms of the security document and make a decision on whether the appointment can proceed under the fixed legal charge or under the Law of Property Act 1925 which is considered in detail below.

Options for a Borrower

1.37. Borrowers would be well advised to obtain professional advice when faced with formal or informal notification of default or on receipt of a reservation of rights letter. In many situations, there will be some communication with the lender and a window of opportunity whereby the borrower may be able to come to a negotiated arrangement with the lender to prevent formal action being taken. This may range from the lender agreeing to exercise forbearance for a period of time, to agreeing a plan and timescales for full redemption of the secured debt, whether by way of sale or refinancing.

1.38. Solicitors may be engaged to act on behalf of borrowers in relation to these pre-action communications or negotiations. The borrower's solicitors will need to review the facility documents to ascertain what events of default have occurred and what other rights or powers the lender may have under the facility documents. It is recommended that borrowers attempt to engage with lenders with the aim of reaching an amicable solution and also to ensure that the lender correctly complies with the requirements of the facility documents in relation to notice provisions and timescales. The borrower's adviser will need to decide if, when and how to notify the lender of any breaches of obligation on the lender's part, depending on the consequences the breach may have on the action the lender proposes to take and/or the stage of the negotiations between the parties. Sharing the progress of a potential sale, such as the receipt of offers and prospective purchasers committing to the process by e.g. undertaking searches, may comfort the lender.

1.39. If the borrower makes proposals to the lender regarding sale, refinancing or some other payment arrangement, then suitable evidence should be provided to the lender to support the proposal. If there is no realistic refinancing, other payment arrangement or non-financial proposals that assuage the lender's concerns or cure the events of default, then borrowers should consider whether it is beneficial to them to work towards a swift termination of the relationship. This may involve a sale of the secured property. Lenders may be willing to allow the borrower to control the marketing and sale, if suitable timescales are agreed, together with a clear plan as to how that is to be achieved. For example, the procurement of professional valuations and appointment of marketing and sale agents.

1.40. Borrowers often wish to retain control of a sale in the belief that they will achieve a higher sale price and/or at lower cost, than if they rescinded control of the sale to the lender or receivers.

1.41. Borrowers and their advisers should have regard to the lender's contractual indemnity in relation to costs. Most facility agreements will entitle the lender to recover their costs from borrowers, whether by way of demand, indemnity or by debiting to the secured debt. These will likely include the cost of the lender's legal and other professional advisers, often on the condition that such costs are reasonably incurred. Proportionality must be maintained as it will not be in the borrower's financial interests to meet its own direct legal costs, and the lender's costs, incurred in negotiations or disputes.

This will depend in large part on the financial standing of the borrower and the value of the borrower's debt against the current value of the security.

Fixed Charge vs LPA Receiverships

1.42. A key distinction in the field of receivership concerns receivers appointed under the terms of a fixed legal charge (known as fixed charge receivers) on the one hand, and receivers appointed pursuant to the Law of Property Act 1925 (known as "LPA receivers", or "Law of Property Act receivers") on the other hand.

1.43. Fundamentally, fixed charge receivership is a contractual mechanism. The formalities and method of appointment and the powers of the receivers are determined by the contractual terms contained in the security documents or mortgage conditions, whereas a Law of Property Act receiver is a creature of statute in terms of the formalities of appointment and the powers granted to the receiver, which are limited.

1.44. It is not unusual for there to be overlapping provisions in several of the security documents, for example, provisions in a legal charge and further provisions in mortgage terms and conditions. If that is the case, it is necessary to carefully review the documents to understand which provisions will take priority.

Statutory conditions for Law of Property Act receivers

1.45. A lender under a legal charge or mortgage has a statutory right to appoint a receiver pursuant to section 101(1)(iii) of the Law of Property Act 1925:

(1) A mortgagee, where the mortgage is made by deed, shall, by virtue of this Act, have the following powers, to the like extent as if they had been in terms conferred by the mortgage deed, but not further (namely):

...

(iii) A power, when the mortgage money has become due, to appoint a receiver of the income of the mortgaged property, or any part thereof; or, if the mortgaged property consists of an interest in income, or of a rentcharge or an annual or other periodical sum, a receiver of that property or any part thereof...

1.46. There are therefore two statutory conditions. Firstly, this power arises when "*the mortgage money has become due*". The terms of the mortgage must be reviewed carefully to ascertain when the mortgage money becomes due. Some mortgage terms provide for the mortgage money to become due on the date of the mortgage, but some conditions state that the money is only due following a defined event of default, or on demand after an event of default.

1.47. When the money is due on the date of the mortgage, the appointment of the receiver can be made immediately after completion of the mortgage. If, however, there are contractual conditions, then these must be met before the right to appoint a receiver arises.

1.48. If a demand is required, the mortgage terms should be checked to ascertain if there are any contractual requirements as to what the demand must contain and any requirements as to service of the demand.

1.49. A demand must clearly state that the mortgage balance is due immediately and it is recommended to state the mortgage balance, noting that the figure provided is not a redemption figure if necessary.[14]

1.50. If there are no contractual requirements as to service of the demand, then it is best practice to effect service by process server. It is not necessary for the demand to be acknowledged by the borrower or recipient, but it is recommended to obtain a written acknowledgement, if possible, particularly if a process server is not being utilised.

1.51. When the borrower is a deceased person, the demand should be served on the personal representative or the Public Trustee, as appropriate.

1.52. The borrower should be provided with a short period of time in which to pay the sum demanded before receivers are appointed. Unless the borrower has confirmed to the lender that he cannot or will not satisfy the demand, in which case an appointment can be made immediately after the demand has been served.

1.53. The second statutory condition states that the lender must be "*entitled to exercise the power of sale*" which occurs when at least one of the conditions set out in Section 103 of the Law of Property Act 1925 is met:

> *(i) Notice requiring payment of the mortgage money has been served on the mortgagor or one of two or more mortgagors, and default has been made in payment of the mortgage*

---

14 A redemption figure is typically the final settlement figure which may include additional costs and interest and be valid for payment for a specified period of time. It is often different from the "running" balance which may not include costs and interest

money, or of part thereof, for three months after such service; or

(ii) Some interest under the mortgage is in arrear and unpaid for two months after becoming due; or

(iii) There has been a breach of some provision contained in the mortgage deed or in this Act, or in an enactment replaced by this Act, and on the part of the mortgagor, or of some person concurring in making the mortgage, to be observed or performed, other than and besides a covenant for payment of the mortgage money or interest thereon.

1.54. Mortgage conditions will typically set out a list of pre-defined events, the occurrence of which will permit the lender to appoint receivers or take other enforcement action. These are commonly referred to as "trigger points" and must be carefully reviewed and construed. Common trigger points include: mortgage arrears, sometimes of a specified amount or duration e.g. two months' worth of arrears; a breach of any condition in the mortgage or mortgage offer; where other occupational or security interests are created without the lender's consent; insolvency action against the borrower,[15] there is a breach of any statutory requirements, and there is a breach of any leasehold covenants if the property is leasehold.

1.55. Where the borrower is bankrupt and the mortgage conditions allow the lender to appoint receivers if the borrower is declared bankrupt, the lender is not entitled to appoint receivers on this ground alone, without the leave of the court. This restriction is set out in section 110 of the Law of Property Act 1925.[16]

---

15 See paragraph 1.55 in relation to insolvency action

16 See paragraph 2.15 to 2.18 in relation to bankruptcy

Summary

1.56. Prior to the appointment of receivers, lenders should consider the merits of commissioning a security review to ascertain the enforceability of the security and outline options, together with a Receiver Pre-appointment report in complex or high value cases.

1.57. A good security review will carefully assess the enforceability of the security and set out the results of searches in relation to the position of the borrower, outline the type of receivership options available (fixed charge receivers vs Law of Property Act receiver) and the powers of the receiver. Any issues, risks or deficiencies should be highlighted.

1.58. Once receivership is determined to be the appropriate enforcement option, it is necessary to carefully consider the contractual terms contained in the security documentation or mortgage conditions. This is to ascertain the specific circumstances in which a fixed charge receiver can be appointed and any pre-conditions of appointment (such as the service of a demand).

CHAPTER TWO

APPOINTMENT

2. Introduction

2.1. This chapter considers how a lender will go about making a receiver appointment. There are a number of restrictions on who can act as a receiver and consideration must be given to the status of the various parties – the lender, the receivers and the borrower – with regard to solvency status and death.

2.2. Once the lender makes the decision that it wishes to appoint receivers, the necessary formalities to make the appointment need to be carefully followed. There are rules around the acceptance of certain receiver appointments and then tasks that the receiver must attend to after the appointment has been made.

Who can appoint a receiver?

2.3. The power to appoint a receiver[17] sits with a lender either under the powers conferred by a fixed legal charge or under section 101 of the Law of Property Act 1925.[18]

2.4. As detailed in Chapter 1, a secured lender has the power to appoint a receiver either under section 101 of the Law of Property Act 1925 or under the terms of a fixed legal charge. In practice is it common for these rights to be in parallel or

---

17 Administrative receivers, agricultural receivers and Court appointed receivers are outside the scope of this work

18 See paragraph 1.45

overlapping such that a mortgagee can elect to make an appointment under the Law of Property Act 1925 or under the fixed legal charge.

2.5. The right to appoint a receiver is not limited to the original lender, but also to its successors in title under section 114 of the Law of Property Act 1925 unless there are contractual restrictions on assignment contained in the mortgage terms. In practice, it is common for mortgages to be transferred from the original lender to a subsequent lender and sometimes this happens repeatedly. The lender with the power to appoint a receiver is the lender who is the current proprietor of the legal charge and not a previous proprietor. Under section 58(1) of the Land Registration Act 2002, the registered proprietor of a legal estate is deemed to have it vested in him, and a legal charge or mortgage is classed as a legal estate.[19]

2.6. Subsequent mortgagees, who are assignees of the original mortgage, are bound by the terms incorporated into the original mortgage.

2.7. Similarly, mortgagees who are foreign registered companies or individuals, whether they are domiciled in England & Wales or elsewhere, also have the power to appoint receivers because the power is derived solely from the existence of the mortgage.

2.8. Different rules apply to equitable mortgages, depending on the nature of the equitable mortgage. Under an equitable mortgage or equitable charge created by deed, the lender will have the contractual powers provided for in the mortgage agreement and the powers set out in section 101 of the Law of

[19] See section 132(1), 1(2)(c) and (4) of the Law of Property Act 1925

Property Act 1925, including the power to appoint a receiver[20].

2.9. If the equitable mortgage is not created by deed, then the lender will not have the powers contained in section 101 of the Law of Property 1925, including the statutory power to appoint a receiver. The lender will have the benefit of contractual powers contained in the mortgage agreement if capable of being granted by simple contract as opposed to a deed.

Effect of Bankruptcy, Liquidation, Dissolution and Death

Lender

2.10. Following the appointment of an administrator, a company lender may only appoint receivers with the consent of the administrator under paragraph 64(1), Schedule B1 of the Insolvency Act 1986 and the power to execute the appointment document under paragraph 9, Schedule 1 of the Insolvency Act 1986.

2.11. Following the appointment of a liquidator, a company lender may only appoint receivers acting by the liquidator pursuant to paragraph 7, Schedule 4 of the Insolvency Act 1986 or through the consent mechanism at section 103 or section 91(2) of the Insolvency Act 1986 as the case may be.

2.12. With regard to a bankrupt individual lender, there are no provisions analogous with the position of a liquidator or administrator, although section 306 of the Insolvency Act 1986 states that the bankruptcy estate, which would include any legal charge, vests in the trustee in bankruptcy or the

[20] under section 101(1)(iii) of the Law of Property Act 1925

official receiver immediately on appointment. There is some debate over whether an individual lender would lose the power to appoint a fixed charge or Law of Property Act receiver. Given that the vast majority of mortgage lenders are companies, this may be a rare occurrence in practice.

2.13. If the company lender is dissolved and ceases to exist, the mortgage as an asset would devolve to the Crown under the bona vacantia process and there would be no ability to appoint receivers because the lender would not exist.

2.14. When an individual lender dies, the personal representatives acting under a grant of probate or letters of administration, can appoint receivers.

Borrower

2.15. When a company borrower is dissolved the mortgage security, and the ability to appoint receivers survives.[21] Ownership of the secured property itself will pass to the Crown as bona vacantia. This does not generally affect the ability of a mortgage lender to appoint receivers or of receivers to discharge their duties but communication with the Crown's representatives is recommended.[22] The Crown may elect, or be asked, to disclaim the property. When a borrower company in administration, no step may be taken to enforce security over the company's property (which would include the appointment of receivers) without the consent of the

21 Note that the pre-conditions of appointment will need to be carefully checked for any complications. For example, if a receiver appointment can only be made once a demand has been served and is unsatisfied, it may be necessary to restore the borrower company such that a demand can be validly served, before an appointment can be made.

22 See https://www.gov.uk/government/organisations/bona-vacantia

administrator or the permission of the court pursuant to paragraph 43(a), Schedule B1 of the Insolvency Act 1986.

2.16. When a company borrower is in liquidation or subject to a winding up order, there is an automatic stay on actions or proceedings concerning company property, which will include the appointment of receivers, except with leave of the court. It has been held that a mortgage lender, as a secured creditor, will usually succeed in lifting the stay to enable enforcement of the mortgage.[23]

2.17. Leave of the court is also required to appoint receivers over a company in liquidation where the ground for appointment is solely due to the liquidation, pursuant to section 110 and 205(1)(i) of the Law of Property Act 1925.

2.18. The bankruptcy of an individual borrower does not prohibit a secured lender from appointing receivers. However, leave from the court will be required if the sole reason for the appointment is due to the bankruptcy itself under section 110 of the Law of Property Act 1925. Lenders should also be aware of the rules concerning disclosing the security in a proof.[24]

Who can act as a receiver?

2.19. It is advisable for a lender to appoint suitably qualified and experienced receivers. Although receivers are not a regulated or restricted profession, they tend to come from either insolvency or surveying backgrounds and may be subject to professional regulation depending on their qualifications or practising status. There is a trade association serving the property

---

23 *Nordic Trustee A.S.A. v OGX Petróleo e Gás S.A.* [2016] EWHC 25 (Ch) at paragraph 50

24 See Rule 14.16 of The Insolvency (England and Wales) Rules 2016

receivership community – the Association of Property and Fixed Charge Receivers, known as NARA, which maintains a membership directory and provides a certified training and qualification regime.

2.20. There are few legal limitations on who can be appointed to act as a receiver.

2.21. Section 109(1) of the Law of Property Act 1925 permits a lender to appoint "*such persons as he thinks fit*" to be a receiver. Case law has provided some limited guidelines: the lender is under a duty of care not to appoint an incompetent person or someone who intends to exercise powers for an improper purpose, although someone connected with the lender can be appointed.[25]

2.22. The mortgage terms may also place restrictions on who can be appointed as a fixed charge receiver, although in practice this may be uncommon.

2.23. Appointments of corporate receivers are not common and section 30 of the Insolvency Act 1986 states "*A body corporate is not qualified for appointment as receiver of the property of a company, and any body corporate which acts as such a receiver is liable to a fine*". Note this relates only to receivers appointed over company borrowers.

2.24. Lenders and receivers would also be well advised to make and accept joint appointments – in other words, an appointment of two individual receivers, rather than an appointment of a single receiver. This has practical benefits of ensuring the receivership can continue if one receiver becomes unable or unwilling to proceed as well as to enable the receivers to benefit

---

[25] *Downsview Nominees Ltd and another v First City Corp Ltd and another* [1993] 3 All ER 626

from the overreaching rights on the sale of the secured property.[26]

2.25. A bankrupt person commits an offence if they act as receiver of company property pursuant to section 31(2) of the Insolvency Act 1986, although there is no such restriction applying to individual borrowers. Similarly, a person subject to a disqualification order cannot act as a receiver of company property without leave of the court.[27]

Making the Appointment

2.26. The appointment of a receiver is a three-step process: firstly, the appointing lender will execute an appointment document; secondly, the executed appointment document will be delivered to the receivers; and thirdly, the receivers will accept the appointment.

Appointment document

2.27. There are statutory requirements in the Law of Property Act 1925 which must be followed for a Law of Property Act receiver appointment to be valid: the lender must appoint the receiver "*by writing under his hand*"[28] but the appointment does not need to be made by deed.

2.28. There may also be requirements contained within the legal charge or incorporated mortgage terms, which must be complied with if the appointment of a fixed charge receiver is to be valid. If there are no contractual provisions in the legal

26 See HM Land Registry Practice Guide 36A, para 5

27 See sections 1 and 22 of the Company Directors Disqualification Act 1986 and section 1170A of the Companies Act 2006

28 Section 109(1) of the Law of Property Act 1925

charge or mortgage terms, then the statutory provisions should be adhered to.

2.29. A lender can elect whether to make an appointment solely under the Law of Property Act 1925, in which case it is only the statutory requirements that must be met. Or they may make an appointment under the fixed charge, in which case the contractual requirements must be met. In practice, a receiver appointment will often be drafted so as to cover both, such that the receiver can exercise both the statutory powers and more extensive contractual powers.

2.30. In order to comply with the requirement for the lender to appoint the receivers "*by writing under his hand*"[29], it is prudent to ensure that the appointment document is signed in wet ink by an individual lender, or by an authorised signatory of a corporate lender or by way of corporate seal.

2.31. It is common in practice for appointments to be signed by way of an electronic signature. It is suggested that this may give rise to a risk that electronic execution is not by writing "*under his hand*" and may therefore be invalid. In order to avoid this risk, a wet ink signature or corporate seal is recommended.

2.32. As noted above, the appointment does not have to be by deed unless the legal charge or mortgage terms require it. However, a deed may be preferable because it will enable the receivers to execute deeds on behalf of the mortgagor, whether or not there is a power of attorney. The downside with making an appointment by deed is that the formalities of execution need to be complied with, which are more burdensome for the lender.

---

[29] Section 109(1) of the Law of Property Act 1925

2.33. There is no prescribed form of appointment. It is recommended to include the following provisions in an appointment document:

- Name and address of lender and company registration number if it is a corporate lender
- Name and address of the borrower and company registration number if it is a corporate borrower
- Name and business address(es) of receiver(s) and whether they are appointed jointly
- Description, address and title number of the secured properties – often these are listed in a schedule to the appointment document
- Description and date of the legal charge
- Explanation of whether the appointment is made under the Law of Property Act 1925 and/or powers contained in the fixed legal charge
- Whether the receivers are to be deemed agent of the borrower
- A summary of the receivers' powers by reference to the Law of Property Act 1925 and/or the fixed legal charge and what powers the lender is delegating to the receivers
- The date of any demand issued by the lender and summary of the events of default/grounds on which the appointment is made
- The date of the notice of appointment

- Where the appointment is being signed by an individual lender, or by an authorised signatory on behalf of a corporate lender, the name and title of the signatory with a space for them to add their wet ink signature.

2.34. It is recommended to either annex a separate form of acceptance for the receivers to sign or include a section within the appointment for the receivers to countersign to confirm their acceptance.

Delivery of the appointment document

2.35. An appointment must be served on the receivers for it to be a valid appointment.

2.36. There are no statutory requirements as to service of the appointment document. The fixed legal charge should be reviewed to ascertain whether there are service requirements concerning a receiver appointment.

2.37. It is common in practice for executed appointment documents to be served on the receivers by post and email. If the appointment is made by deed, the formalities of delivery will need to be complied with.[30]

2.38. It is recommended for the lender to make enquiries with the receivers in advance of the appointment document being served to ascertain their availability to sign and accept the appointment. This is particularly important in relation to appointments concerning company borrowers.[31]

30 Section 1(2) of the Law of Property (Miscellaneous Provisions) Act 1989 and Section 46 of the Companies Act 2006

31 See paragraph 2.39 regarding acceptance

Acceptance

2.39. An appointment must be accepted by the receivers for it to be a valid appointment.[32]

2.40. Receivers should be advised to ensure that they have appropriate insurance cover in place before accepting an appointment. In practice, most receivers will have a block insurance policy in place, but any notification provisions in such a policy will need to be followed.[33]

2.41. There is no prescribed form of acceptance but any requirements in the fixed legal charge should be complied with.

2.42. It is recommended that the receivers either countersign the appointment document or sign a separate acceptance document or letter and issue it to the lender.

2.43. In relation to corporate borrowers only, the appointment must be accepted by the receiver "*before the end of the business day next following that on which the instrument of appointment is received by him or on his behalf*".[34] And the appointment is deemed to be made at the time at which the appointment document was received.[35] These statutory provisions do not apply to borrowers who are individual persons.

2.44. There are further statutory requirements in relation the acceptance of appointments concerning corporate borrowers. Rule 4.1(4) of The Insolvency (England and Wales) Rules

---

32 *RA Cripps (Pharmaceutical) and Son Ltd v Wickenden* [1973] 1 WLR 944

33 See paragraph 3.21 regarding insurance

34 Section 33(1)(a) of the Insolvency Act 1986

35 Section 33(1)(b) of the Insolvency Act 1986

2016 requires the following to be noted on the acceptance document:

- Name and address of lender
- Name and address of receivers
- Name of the company borrower (note that these requirements do not apply to individual borrowers)
- Time and date of receipt of the appointment document by the receivers
- Time and date of the receiver's acceptance of the appointment

2.45. The requirements above need to be complied with within 5 business days of the acceptance.[36]

2.46. So in practice, a receiver has until the end of the business day following the day on which the appointment was received to accept it. That acceptance can be verbal or by conduct. The receiver then has until the end of 5 business days from the date of acceptance to confirm the acceptance in writing to the lender following the requirements in Rule 4.1 of The Insolvency (England and Wales) Rules 2016.

2.47. The written confirmation of acceptance must be sent to the lender, although there are no statutory requirements for methods of service.

2.48. There are no such formalities for acceptance of appointments concerning individual borrowers. Nevertheless, it is

[36] Rule 4.1(3) of The Insolvency (England and Wales) Rules 2016

recommended that receivers prepare a written acceptance to include the information noted above and send it to the lender, although note there are no statutory time limits for acceptance or providing confirmation of acceptance to the lender.

Verification Report

2.49. It is common practice for receivers to require a verification report[37] from their solicitors immediately following acceptance, or sometimes in parallel with their appointment. A verification report is not a statutory requirement. The purpose of the report is for receivers to obtain advice that their appointment is "valid" and that they can therefore undertake the performance of their duties without fear of acting ultra vires and incurring personal liability.[38]

2.50. The content of a verification report will vary depending on the requirements of the receivers. Advisers should check whether their receivers require the report to cover any specific points or be in a certain format. Absent any specific instructions, it is recommended that the following points are covered in a verification report:

- Details of appointing lender and the borrower

- Details of the charge under which the receivers are appointed, including, the names of the parties, whether any of the original parties differ, and the date of the charge

37 Sometimes called a validation report or validation advice

38 See paragraphs 2.86 regarding defective and invalid appointments

- Confirmation that the charge is registered in the Charges Register of the secured property at HM Land Registry and its ranking priority

- Details of any other priority or subservient registered chargeholders or restriction holders

- Confirmation that any necessary pre-appointment conditions were met and that the receivers' appointment is valid[39] and the date the appointment was made and the date it was accepted

- A summary of the powers granted to the receivers under the legal charge, together with references to the specific clause within the charge or mortgage conditions with advice on any common powers that are missing

- If the property is leasehold, details of the lease (such as the parties and the remaining term)

- Details of any title errors, issues or risk (for example, if the address of the secured property contained in the mortgage deed differs from the address contained in the Property Register within the HM Land Registry Title).

2.51. If there are particular issues or risks, it may be prudent for receivers to be advised to obtain further detailed or specialist advice, for example, by way of a full title report in relation to title issues.[40]

---

39 See paragraph 2.26 regarding making an appointment

40 It is reasonably common in practice for receivers to instruct the same solicitors as those who acted for the lender, subject to the usual professional obligations around managing potential conflicts of interest.

Post-Appointment Tasks

2.52. There are a number of tasks that should be attended to immediately following the acceptance of the appointment.

Notice to borrower

2.53. Absent any requirements in the legal charge, there is no statutory requirement for the lender or the receiver to notify the borrower that receivers have been appointed.

2.54. It is, however, advisable for receivers to notify the borrower in writing that they have been appointed, confirm the date of the appointment, provide the borrower with a copy of the appointment document and outline the purpose of the receivership and the receivers' powers and obligations. The receivers should ask for the borrower's cooperation and for the provision of useful information that will assist the receivers in discharging their duties, such as:

- Details of who is in occupation of the property, on what terms and when they gained occupation

- Copies of any leases, sub-leases, occupation agreements, statutory notices (such as tenancy deposit scheme details for residential properties) and statements of rental accounts

- Details of any other relevant contractual relationships, such as managing agents appointed by the borrower to

---

Some receivers may seek separate representation, particularly in high-risk cases. Appropriate solicitor/client engagement letters will need to be issued in all cases manage the property, or if the secured property is leasehold the managing agents appointed by the landlord.

2.55. Receivers and their advisers should bear in mind that most borrowers have no experience of receivership or even a basic understanding of the concept. Some borrowers will offer no engagement, and others may be actively obstructive. The work of the receivers can be significantly eased if borrowers cooperate with the receivers. This can lead to lower receivership costs, so the provision of adequate information to the borrower is recommended; effective communication is a two-way process.

2.56. Once the documentation is obtained, receivers will need to carefully consider the rights, obligations and liabilities contained therein, noting that receivers should take active steps to manage the charged property, for example, by considering any rent reviews affecting leasehold property.[41]

<u>Notice to occupiers</u>

2.57. Receivers should provide prompt written notice to tenants and occupiers of their appointment, although there is no statutory requirement to do so.

2.58. In practical terms, the receivers will require information from the tenants or occupiers to allow the receivers to properly consider how to design a strategy to meet their duties to the lender.[42]

2.59. The receivers should request:

---

41 See *Silven Properties Limited v Royal Bank of Scotland* [2003] EWCA Civ 1409

42 See Chapter 4 regarding receiver duties

- Details of who is in occupation of the property, on what terms and when they gained occupation

- Copies of any leases, sub-leases, occupation agreements, statutory notices (such as tenancy deposit details for residential properties) and rent demands

- Details of who rent is paid to and when e.g. weekly, monthly, quarterly and on what date

- Details of any other relevant relationships, such as managing agents

- Details of any gas safety certificates or other such information depending on the type and use of the property

2.60. The receivers should explain to tenants and occupiers who appointed them and what their role is.

2.61. The borrower can continue to give valid receipts to tenants in relation to rent payments until the receivers notify the tenant of their appointment and provide new details for the collection of rent.

2.62. However, before doing so, it is important for receivers to understand that basis of the tenants' or occupiers' occupation and make a decision on whether to accept their status, before demanding or collecting rent. This is because demanding or collecting rent from occupiers may inadvertently provide occupiers with rights of occupation that the receivers may later not want to accept. It is only when the receivers are satisfied as to the occupiers' right to occupation, that rent should be demanded and accepted. There may be ways of mitigating risk in these circumstances, for example, if the lender or receivers do wish to collect money they may require the occupiers to maintain a separate account for rent, or by accepting money on the basis it is for mesne profits.[43]

Notice to Companies House

2.63. In relation to a corporate borrower, the receivers have a statutory obligation to provide notice of the appointment to the Registrar of Companies.[44] It is debateable whether receivers are required to provide this notice if they are only appointed as Law of Property Act receivers (rather than under a fixed charge)[45] but it is recommended to do so regardless, so as to minimise any risk of criminal liability under the Act.

2.64. Notice to the Registrar should be given in the prescribed form, using Companies House Form RM01.[46] A failure to meet this requirement creates criminal liability for a fine. Following receipt of the Notice, the Registrar will publish it on the public companies register.[47]

---

43 See also *Paratus AMC Ltd v Persons Unknown* [2012] EWHC 3791 (Ch) in which payments made to, and accepted by, a mortgage lender by a tenant in occupation under a tenancy which post-dated the mortgage did not amount to an assurance or representation or encouragement of the sort giving rise to an estoppel or waiver

44 Section 859K of the Companies Act 2006

45 Section 859K(1)(b) of the Companies Act 2006 applies when a lender "*appoints such a receiver or manager under powers contained in an instrument*" and no express reference is made to a statutory appointment under the Law of Property Act 1925

46 https://www.gov.uk/government/publications/appoint-an-administrative-receiver-receiver-or-manager-rm01

47 https://find-and-update.company-information.service.gov.uk/

HM Land Registry

2.65. *Practice Guide 36A: receivers appointed under the provisions of the Law of Property Act 1925* provides guidance to practitioners following the appointment of receivers.[48] The property remains vested in the borrower and the borrower will remain the registered proprietor of the property; the receivers will not become the registered proprietor or otherwise have their appointment noted on the title register.

2.66. Receivers should consider using the statutory mechanism to change the borrower's address for service or adding their own address as a secondary service address, as a means of providing indirect notice to third parties and to ensure relevant correspondence is sent to the receivers rather than the borrower.[49]

2.67. The procedure is set out in *Practice Guide 65A*. In short, the receivers must send to HM Land Registry a form AP1, a certified copy of the receiver's appointment together with evidence that the receiver has power to apply on behalf of the borrower, and a certified copy of the mortgage (if it is not already registered or noted). No fee is payable.

2.68. Note that at the end of the receivership, the receiver's address will need to be removed but this will only take place if the registered proprietor has another address for service.[50]

---

48 https://www.gov.uk/government/publications/dispositions-executed-by-law-of-property-act-receivers/practice-guide-36a-receivers-appointed-under-the-provisions-of-the-law-of-property-act-1925

49 See Rule 198 of The Land Registration Rules 2003

50 See https://www.gov.uk/government/publications/dispositions-executed-by-law-of-property-act-receivers/practice-guide-36a-receivers-appointed-under-the-provisions-of-the-law-of-property-act-1925

Other Receiver Tasks and Notice to third parties

2.69. It is common for receivers to arrange a visit to the secured property shortly after their appointment, although there is no legal requirement to do so.

2.70. Receivers should also consider the requirement to open an account and contact all relevant authorities and service providers, depending on the type and location of the property. A non-exhaustive list is outlined below:

- Utility providers serving the property
- Local authority
- HM Revenue & Customs[51]
- Other registered charge holders noted on the Charges Register at HM Land Registry

2.71. Receivers appointed over corporate borrowers must also comply with the provisions of section 39(1) of the Insolvency Act 1986 which makes provisions for notification:

39 Notification that receiver or manager appointed.

(1) Where a receiver or manager of the property of a company has been appointed—

(a) every invoice, order for goods or services, business letter or order form (whether in hard copy, electronic or any other form) issued by or on behalf of the company or the receiver or manager or the liquidator of the company; and

---

[51] See paragraph 4.19 regarding HMRC and VAT considerations

(b) all the company's websites,

must contain a statement that a receiver or manager has been appointed.

(2) If default is made in complying with this section, the company and any of the following persons, who knowingly and wilfully authorises or permits the default, namely, any officer of the company, any liquidator of the company and any receiver or manager, is liable to a fine.

Indemnities

2.72. Although section 109(2) of the Law of Property Act 1925 states that the borrower "*shall be solely responsible for the receiver's acts or defaults*" and mortgage conditions will generally include analogous provisions, there are circumstances where receivers may seek a contractual indemnity from the lender.

2.73. A contractual indemnity given by the lender to the receivers will typically serve to indemnify the receivers from and against any losses, claims, liabilities, damages, costs and other expenses incurred by him during and after the end of the appointment, subject to the receivers discharging their duties to the correct standard.

2.74. Contractual indemnities are commonly requested by receivers, and provided by lenders, where there are increased risks or a potential defect in the charge, its registration or the appointment.

2.75. In relation to a company borrower, section 34 of the Insolvency Act 1986 empowers the court to order the appointing lender to indemnify the receiver "*against any liability which arises solely by reason of the invalidity of the appointment*". Receivers may make an application to court in reliance upon this provision if, for example, a lender is unwilling to provide a contractual indemnity in relation to an invalid or defective appointment. There are no parallel provisions for individual borrowers.

Remuneration

Rate of remuneration

2.76. Requirements and restrictions on the receivers' remuneration are set out in the Law of Property Act 1925, which are commonly varied or excluded by the mortgage conditions.

2.77. Section 109(6) of the Law of Property Act 1925 states:

> *109 (6) The receiver shall be entitled to retain out of any money received by him, for his remuneration, and in satisfaction of all costs, charges, and expenses incurred by him as receiver, a commission at such rate, not exceeding five per centum on the gross amount of all money received, as is specified in his appointment, and if no rate is so specified, then at the rate of five per centum on that gross amount, or at such other rate as the court thinks fit to allow, on application made by him for that purpose.*

2.78. The statutory rate of remuneration covers the receivers' time costs and any expenses and disbursements, save where there are specific statutory provisions.

2.79. If the mortgage conditions contain provisions regarding remuneration, these must be carefully followed.

2.80. In practical terms, the receiver should agree terms of their remuneration and an indemnity from the lender for payment of any expenses, costs or disbursements, with the lender prior to an appointment being made or accepted and ensure that the mortgage conditions permit such an arrangement. Remuneration arrangements commonly agreed between lender and received include a percentage of the price at which the secured property is sold but may also include provisions of payment of hourly rates and payment of all costs and expenses incurred by the receivers.

2.81. The receivers have the right to make an application to court for the court to set a rate of remuneration "*as the court thinks fit to allow*" but this is unusual in practice.[52]

2.82. Liquidators of a corporate borrower in liquidation can make an application to court to fix the remuneration of a fixed charge receiver and thereby alter the statutory or contractual provisions as to renumeration, which can then be varied by the receivers on application.[53]

Accounts and record keeping

2.83. Receivers have a duty to keep accounts.[54] There are also additional obligations on receivers of a corporate borrower to keep accounts of receipts and payments and deliver such

---

52 Section 109(6) of the Law of Property Act 1925

53 Section 36(1) of the Insolvency Act 1986). Receivers can then apply to vary or amend any order made see section 36(3) Insolvency Act 1986

54 *Kennedy v Lyell* (1889) 14 App Cas 437, 59 LJQB 268, 38 WR 353, 62 LT 77

accounts to the Registrar of Companies within the timescales specified in section 38 of the Insolvency Act 1986.[55]

Implied duties regarding remuneration

2.84. The court has implied a number of duties in relation to receivers' remuneration: firstly, a contractual discretion to set terms of remuneration must be exercised in good faith; and secondly, costs, expenses and disbursements, even under a full indemnity, should be reasonably and properly incurred and reasonable in amount.[56]

Acting for borrowers – remuneration

2.85. Borrowers are in principle able to challenge the remuneration charged by receivers and any claim should be based on evidence that the receivers have either acted outside the parameters of the statutory requirements (such as section 109 of the Law of Property Act 1925) or the provisions of the mortgage conditions (whichever apply in the circumstances) and, or in the alternative, that the receivers' implied duties have been breached.[57]

Defective and Invalid Appointments

2.86. The potential consequences to receivers acting under appointments which are defective or invalid are significant.

2.87. An invalid appointment is one which can have no legal effect, such as where the appointing lender had no power to make the

55 Section 38(2) of the Insolvency Act 1986

56 *Gomba Holdings (UK) Ltd v Minories Finance Ltd (No 2) [1992] 4 All ER 588*

57 *See* Chapter 4 regarding receiver duties

appointment, or if the appointing lender did have the power to make the appointment, but where the contractual or statutory pre-conditions of appointment were not satisfied.[58] For example, if a demand was required to be served before a receiver could be appointed, but no demand was served.

2.88. A situation that can occur in practice is where the lender attempted to appoint receivers based on a breach which it incorrectly believed existed (which would, by itself, render the appointment invalid) but where another breach existed which would have allowed the lender to make a valid appointment. It is suggested that such situations should be treated with caution and the specific requirements and "trigger points" set out in the mortgage conditions ought to be carefully considered to ascertain whether the appointment is sound. If there is any doubt and if practicable, it may be wise to terminate the questionable appointment and make a new, valid appointment.

2.89. An appointment will be defective where the appointing lender had the power to make the appointment, and the pre-conditions were met, but where there is a defect in making the appointment. For example, the formalities of making the appointment have not been complied with. Please refer to Chapter 7 for consideration of challenges that can be made against receivers, including where the appointment is defective or invalid.

Summary

2.90. When a lender has made a decision to appoint receivers, it will need to determine whether the appointment is under the Law of Property Act 1925 or the powers contained in a fixed legal

[58] See Chapter 1 regarding pre-conditions of appointment

charge. In either case, it is necessary to ensure that any pre-conditions of appointment are satisfied.

2.91. It is sensible to approach receivers in advance of an appointment being made to discuss the prospective appointment with them and remuneration arrangements. The appointment document itself must then be prepared, ensuring any contractual requirements as to the form and content of the appointment are complied with.

2.92. Once validly executed by the lender, the appointment document will need to be served on the receiver. The receivers must then accept the appointment and it is preferable to do this in writing, ensuring that any statutory timescales and other provisions are complied with for company borrowers. Receivers should then obtain a verification report confirming the validity of the appointment and advice on their powers and any notable legal issues or risks. Receivers should consider whether there are factors which would justify requesting a contractual indemnity from the lender.

2.93. The receivership is then underway and the receivers must begin their work to issue any necessary notices to third parties and take the necessary practical steps. This may include contacting the borrower, occupiers, visiting the secured property and opening accounts.

CHAPTER THREE

POWERS

3. Introduction

3.1. In practice, the extent of receiver powers is often one of the most misunderstood issues in receivership, particularly the power of receivers to act as agent of the borrower.

3.2. The powers enjoyed by receivers are variable. Receivers appointed under the Law of Property Act 1925 have a relatively limited set of powers, the principal power being to collect income from the secured property (the origin of the term receiver emanating from the power to *receive* income).

3.3. Receivers appointed under a fixed legal charge will ordinarily have a wider range of powers, which are described in, and granted by, the contractual terms in the mortgage or facility agreement. The lender may also delegate or donate certain of its powers to receivers.

3.4. A fundamental principle of receivership concerns the agency between the receivers and the borrower – a power enabling receivers to act as agent for the borrower. They may also act as agent for the lender in certain circumstances or otherwise have a right to exercise powers of a lender without acting as the lender's agent.

3.5. This chapter considers powers granted to the receivers by the Law of Property Act 1925 and common powers granted under a fixed legal charge.

Powers under the Law of Property Act 1925

3.6. A receiver appointed solely under the Law of Property Act 1925 will enjoy the powers contained in section 109. These are often referred to as the statutory powers and they are very limited. Notably, the power to sell the secured property is not granted by the Law of Property Act 1925 and it is principally for this reason that most appointments in practice are fixed charge receiver appointments.

<u>Receive Income</u>

3.7. Section 109(3) of the Law of Property Act 1925 states:

> "*The receiver shall have power to demand and recover all the income of which he is appointed receiver, by action or under section 72(1) of the Tribunals, Courts and Enforcement Act 2007 (commercial rent arrears recovery), or otherwise, in the name either of the mortgagor or of the mortgagee, to the full extent of the estate or interest which the mortgagor could dispose of, and to give effectual receipts accordingly for the same, and to exercise any powers which may have been delegated to him by the mortgagee pursuant to this Act.*"

3.8. It is therefore clear that the primary purpose of this provision is to empower the receiver to collect income due to the borrower.

3.9. Section 205(1)(xiv) of the Law of Property Act 1925 states that "'*income' includes rents and profits*".

3.10. Rent paid by tenants is the most obvious source of income that receivers can collect under this provision. The usual requirements as to the provision of demands required by any lease or notices providing prescribed information must be complied with.[59]

3.11. There is authority to indicate that receivers have the power, and arguably an obligation, to exercise any applicable statutory or contractual rent review powers.[60] So it is important for receivers to properly analyse the borrower's leases and understand whether there are rent review provisions and when and how they are to be triggered. Receivers must also have regard to the statutory regime for rent reviews in private rented tenancies which may require recourse to the First-tier Tribunal.[61]

3.12. Other categories of income that could be collected by receivers includes fees paid to occupy the property under a licence, short-term or holiday letting. Receivers can also collect damages from occupiers for occupation of the property or mesne profits or potentially from third parties (such as managing agents) who are collecting rent to which the receivers are entitled by way of a claim for unjust enrichment.[62]

3.13. Receivers acting under the Law of Property Act are entitled to collect income by way of action or litigation.[63]

3.14. Under section 101(1)(iii) of the Law of Property Act 1925 the lender can appoint a receiver "*if the mortgaged property consists*

59 For example, those required by section 47(1) and section 48(1) of the Landlord and Tenant Act 1987

60 *Knight v Lawrence* [1993] BCLC 215

61 See Sections 13 and 14 of the Housing Act 1988 (as amended by section 6 of the Renters' Rights Act 2025)

62 *Official Custodian for Charities v Mackey (No 2)* [1985] 2 All ER 1016

63 Section 109(3) of the Law of Property Act 1925

of an interest in income, or of a rentcharge or an annual or other periodical sum".

Powers delegated by mortgagee under statute – leases and surrenders

3.15. Section 109(3) of the Law of Property Act 1925 states:

> "*The receiver shall have power … to exercise any powers which may have been delegated to him by the mortgagee pursuant to this Act*"

3.16. The lender must expressly delegate such powers to the receiver in writing, either in the mortgage deed or separately.

3.17. The powers that are expressly able to be delegated under the statute are: the power of leasing, and the power to accept surrenders.

3.18. The power to grant leases, delegated by the lender, arises from section 99(19) of the Law of Property Act 1925 which states:

> *The powers of leasing conferred by this section shall, after a receiver of the income of the mortgaged property or any part thereof has been appointed by a mortgagee under his statutory power, and so long as the receiver acts, be exercisable by such mortgagee instead of by the mortgagor, as respects any land affected by the receivership, in like manner as if such mortgagee were in possession of the land, and the mortgagee may, by writing, delegate any of such powers to the receiver.*

3.19. The power to accept surrenders in accordance with section 100(13) of the Law of Property Act 1925, can also be delegated on terms almost identical to section 99(19). As above, the receivers act as agent for the borrower so can accept surrenders in the borrower's name and in the lender's name, provided the lender has granted them the right to do so.

3.20. It is unclear whether the other statutory powers of lenders can be delegated to receivers, such as the lender's statutory power to insure and cut and sell timber from, the secured property.[64]

Insurance

3.21. Receivers appointed under the Law of Property Act 1925 have a limited power and, indeed, an obligation, to take out insurance in relation to the secured property. Section 109(7) of the Law of Property Act 1925 sets out the requirements, namely, that the lender must direct the receivers to insure to the extent that the lender has a power to insure, limited to cover fire damage and paid for out of money collected by the receivers. The insurance should be in the borrower's name with the receivers acting as agent for the borrower pursuant to section 109(2) of the Law of Property Act 1925.[65] The lender's statutory power to take out insurance should also be noted.[66]

Powers under the legal charge

3.22. Fixed charge receivers can be granted more extensive powers than those arising from the Law of Property Act 1925. In practice, most receivers are appointed as fixed charge receivers

64 See paragraph 3.29 regarding the statutory power of sale and paragraph 6.33 regarding the lender's power of sale

65 There are some obvious risks to receivers in relying upon the borrower's insurance policy, even if the receivers are noted on the policy, Specialist advice from insurance brokers or providers should be obtained

66 See section 101(1)(ii) of the Law of Property Act 1925

precisely so they can exercise the more extensive powers usually contained in mortgage conditions.

3.23. It is common for mortgage conditions to state that receivers are granted all of the powers contained in the Law of Property Act 1925 and the additional powers set out within the conditions. These powers may be expressly set out in conditions applicable to receivers, or they may be described as powers enjoyed by the mortgagee but extended to the receivers as well.

3.24. The extent of the powers granted by the mortgage conditions to a fixed charge receiver are a matter of construction and in practice, mortgage conditions must be carefully analysed so as to understand the powers that are granted.

Power to take possession

3.25. The power to take possession of the secured property is, in practical terms, significant. The power is used by receivers with the intention of either managing the property or selling it to redeem the lender's debt. The power to take possession, when exercised correctly, means that any subservient interests (for example, tenancies) can be determined such that the property can be sold with vacant possession in order to maximise its value.

3.26. It is important to consider how the power is granted to the receivers. As we have considered, the power to take possession is not granted by the Law of Property Act 1925. It will either by contained in the mortgage conditions or the lender's power of possession may have been delegated to the receivers in writing, for example in the appointment document or a separate instrument (although the latter is not common in practice).

3.27. A power granted by the mortgage conditions must be construed in accordance with its terms. It is usual for the receivers to act as deemed agent for the borrower and to enter into possession on this basis. Mortgage conditions may also enable the receivers to act as agent for the lender when entering into possession or exercising other powers.[67]

3.28. If the power to take possession is only granted or donated by the lender to the receivers in the appointment document, the receivers will act as the lender's agent and if physical possession of the property is obtained, it will be as agent for the lender. So care must be taken to understand which powers the receivers wish to exercise because that will inform how a claim for possession will be pursued.[68]

Power of sale

3.29. The Law of Property Act 1925 grants lenders a power of sale, but this is not extended to receivers or capable of delegation under the Act.[69] This absence of a statutory power of sale is significant.

3.30. A power of sale must, therefore, be granted to the receiver in the mortgage conditions. It is essential to carefully consider the mortgage conditions to understand if a power of sale is granted to receivers and, if so, the extent of that power or any conditions attaching to it.

3.31. Commonly the power is either granted directly to the receivers in the mortgage conditions or expressly granted to the lender

---

67 See paragraph 3.70 regarding agency powers

68 See Chapter 5 regarding claims for possession

69 Section 101(1)(i) of the Law of Property Act 1925

with the receivers then being granted the same powers as the lender.

3.32. Subject to compliance with the duty to act in good faith, the receivers have the power to decide when and how the secured property is to be sold and options include open market sale, auction sale or pre-pack sale.[70]

Leasing and Surrenders

3.33. As we have seen, sections 99(19) and 100(13) of the Law of Property Act 1925 allow lenders to delegate their power to grant leases and accept surrenders to receivers appointed under the Law of Property Act.

3.34. The provisions of the legal charge and mortgage conditions will be strictly construed and must be carefully considered. They will typically empower receivers to grant leases on terms they think fit, either acting as agent for the borrower and, or in the alternative, acting as donee of a power of attorney.[71]

3.35. Receivers must have regard to any consents that are required, including the consent of the lender (and any subsequent mortgagees) and any restrictions on the provision of that consent. It is common for facility agreements or mortgage offers to contain special conditions containing restrictions on the types of lease or tenancy that the borrower can grant over the secured property, the types of occupier, or the use of the property. If there are difficulties in obtaining consent, it may be possible to exercise the lender's power to grant leases.[72]

---

70 See Chapter 6 regarding sale

71 See paragraph 3.62 regarding powers of attorney

72 See paragraphs 3.68 regarding agency powers

3.36. Similarly, in a leasehold context, the borrower (and receivers acting as agent or attorney for the borrower) will need to comply with any restrictions imposed by lessors and ensure that the necessary consents are obtained.

3.37. Receivers must also have regard to local licencing requirements, for example, relating to selective licencing or leasing.

3.38. The power to accept surrenders will ordinarily be provided in mortgage conditions, in addition to the statutory power referred to above.

Power to carry our repairs

3.39. The receivers' powers to carry out repairs will typically be contained within the mortgage conditions which will be strictly construed.

3.40. Receivers are not under any duty or obligation to carry out repairs in order to improve a secured property, even if conducting repairs or maintenance work will add value such that a higher sale price can be achieved. These are not considerations with which receivers must concern themselves.

3.41. However, receivers may have a statutory obligation to conduct certain repair works. For example, where the property is in a dangerous or unsafe state or poses a threat to others.

3.42. If receivers determine that repair works are necessary or desirable and that conducting such works is within the powers granted to them, it is prudent to obtain the consent of the lender before such expenditure is incurred. If the repair work is more significant, any restrictions in the mortgage terms should be complied with, including obtaining formal lender consent where needed, for example, in relation to structural works.

3.43. In a leasehold context, there may also be restrictions and obligations contained within a lease that must be observed, including requirements to obtain lessor consent.

3.44. Receivers may be empowered by the mortgage conditions to engage contractors as agent for the borrower. If such powers are not contained in the mortgage conditions, the receivers will need to engage contractors in their own right.

Powers and Obligations as a Landlord or Landowner

3.45. Appointed receivers do not, as a matter of course, assume all of the contractual or statutory obligations on a landlord or landowner by virtue of their appointment.

3.46. There are, however, exceptions to the general position. Firstly, if the receivers' contract in their own names, for example, by granting a lease in their own names and not expressly as agent for the borrower. Secondly, if the statute in question can be construed so as to extend obligations on a landlord or landowner to receivers. Thirdly, if there are provisions in the mortgage terms which state that the receivers assume the borrower's liabilities as landlord. This would not be a term one would expect to find in a properly drafted set of mortgage conditions.

3.47. With regard to receivers appointed under the Law of Property Act 1925, there are no provisions within the Act which serve to extend the borrower's contractual or statutory obligations to receivers.

3.48. In practical terms, receivers may wish to comply with obligations placed on landlords by virtue of them acting as agent for the borrower, so that they can exercise appropriate statutory rights. For example, provision of an energy performance certificate to a tenant or prospective purchaser under Regulation 6 The Energy Performance of Buildings (England and Wales) Regulations 2012.

3.49. Numerous statutes impose duties and obligations on landowners or landlords. The guiding principle to apply is to carefully consider the wording of the statute in question to ascertain: (a) on whom the statutory obligation is placed; and (b) whether the receivers may fit the characteristics of that person.

3.50. The number of statutes which place obligations on landowners or landlords are too numerous to list here. However, by way of illustration, some examples can be considered.

3.51. The obligations under of the Defective Premises Act 1972 arguably do not to apply to receivers unless the lease is vested in them because the obligations apply to the "landlord".[73]

3.52. Whereas obligations under the section 4A of the Landlord and Tenant Act 1987 specifically extends the definition of "landlord" to include a "*mortgagee in exercise of a power of sale or leasing*".[74] This wording is arguably sufficient to extend the definition to receivers, despite them not being the "mortgagee".

3.53. Similarly, obligations on a landlord to conduct safety checks in rented accommodation can be construed so as to extend to receivers on the basis that they are, save for the tenancy, entitled to possession:

---

73 Section 4 Defective Premises Act 1972

74 Section 4A of the Landlord and Tenant Act 1987

6.—(1) In this regulation—

"landlord" means—

(a) in England and Wales—

(i) where the relevant premises are occupied under a lease, the person for the time being entitled to the reversion expectant on that lease or who, apart from any statutory tenancy, would be entitled to possession of the premises.[75]

Conducting business and trade

3.54. The role and powers of a receiver principally relate to taking control of a charged asset and achieving its realisation to redeem the secured debt.

3.55. Depending on the circumstances of the borrower and the use of the secured asset, receivers may find a sale of the asset and redemption of the debt difficult to achieve, or there may be other impediments to achieve sale and redemption. One such area encountered in practice is when the charged assets or property is being used for the purposes of operating a business. It may be difficult to divorce the property from the business.

3.56. In such circumstances it is important to consider what powers the receivers have in relation to the business itself.

3.57. The starting point is to consider the extent of the receivers' powers contained in the legal charge and the mortgage conditions, as receivers can only exert control over assets covered by the extent of the legal charge. The wording will need to be carefully construed. The examples of the types of business that receivers may encounter are too numerous to

[75] Regulation 36(1) The Gas Safety (Installation and Use) Regulations 1998

consider in detail and receivers should obtain specialist advice where necessary, having regard to regulatory, planning or licensing restrictions which may apply. Practitioners advising borrowers should carefully consider the extent of the receivers' powers within the legal charge and ascertain whether action being undertaken falls outside of those powers. If receivers act outside of the scope of their powers, action may be taken to restrain them or seek other remedies.[76]

3.58. Receivers have been held to owe a duty of care to borrowers, and others with an interest in the equity of redemption, when managing or operating a borrower's business.[77] The duty is to act as a reasonably competent receiver. Receivers may be liable in damages if that duty is breached and loss is caused.

Employment Considerations

3.59. Receivers may need to consider employees of the borrower where the secured property is used as a business premises and the business remains operational. Specialist employment law advice should be obtained. The precise terms of the receivers' appointment and powers contained in the mortgage conditions must be carefully considered.

3.60. It is likely that the borrower's employment contracts will not be affected by the appointment receivers under a fixed legal charge or the Law of Property Act. The receivers may have powers to enter into new employment contracts, which will likely serve to terminate previous contracts entered into by the borrower with the employee. Note section 37(2) of the Insolvency Act 1986 states that receivers of company borrowers who permit contracts of employment to continue

---

76 See Chapter 7 on challenges

77 *Medforth v Blake* [2000] Ch 86, para 103(B)

for 14 days or more after their appointment will be deemed to have adopted them and will assume personal liability.

3.61. Receivers should also have regard to obligations under The Transfer of Undertakings (Protection of Employment) Regulations 2006 (TUPE). Regulation 3(1)(b) of TUPE applies to services carried out by "a client" on "his own behalf" which are subsequently "carried out instead by another person on the client's behalf". For TUPE to apply, the client must remain the same. It has been held that there could be no service provision change for TUPE purposes in the receivership context where there was a change in contractors (e.g. appointment of new property managers) and also a change of "the client" (e.g. the receivers acting in place of the borrower).

Power of Attorney

3.62. It is common for mortgage conditions to include a power of attorney granted by the borrower to the lender and often this is extended to receivers. The extent of any such power of attorney will be strictly construed. The power of attorney granted in this way typically relates to the execution of documents pertaining to the receivers' appointment. The power of attorney cannot, therefore, be used to assist the receiver in discharging his other duties or exercising other powers.

3.63. The provisions of the Power of Attorney Act 1971 apply, which states:

> Section 1(1) *An instrument creating a power of attorney shall be executed as a deed by the donor of the power.*

3.64. This provision has the effect that powers of attorney granted in a mortgage deed cannot be revoked.

3.65. The bankruptcy or liquidation of a borrower will not terminate a power of attorney given in a security document, despite the receivers' agency being terminated.

3.66. In practical terms, a power of attorney granted in a mortgage deed is often utilised to effect the sale of the secured property or to grant leases.[78]

Powers donated by the Lender

3.67. The lender may donate or delegate certain of its powers to receivers. Such delegation must be contained in the mortgage conditions or the appointment document and see paragraph 3.15 regarding delegation of statutory powers. Such delegation can be a powerful tool, enabling the receivers to act as donee of a power of the lender, rather than being limited to exercising powers as agent of the borrower.

3.68. This is because there are circumstances in which the borrower may be bound by third party interests that the receivers, acting as agent for the borrower, may be unable to terminate. However, the lender will have a "better" position by virtue of its legal estate arising out of the legal charge and the receivers can exercise the lender's power if it is delegated to them.

3.69. A common scenario in practice is where the borrower has granted interests (such as tenancies or leases) in the secured property which he is bound by and which the receivers, acting as the borrower's agent, are also bound by and unable to terminate. But, if the property interests do not bind the lender (for example, if the tenancy or lease granted is a breach of the mortgage conditions) then the receivers may elect to exercise the lender's rights as donees of the lenders power. Note that

78 See Chapter 6 regarding sale

the receivers can act as donee of the lender's powers without acting as agent for the lender.

Agency Powers

3.70. The principles by which receivers act as agent of the borrower are at the heart of receivership and are one of the most powerful tools to restrict the liability of the receivers and the liability of the appointing lender for the receivers' acts. The agency powers enjoyed by receivers are, however, one of the most widely misunderstood topics, differing significantly from the usual common law agency principles and described as having a "special character".[79]

<u>Agent of the Borrower</u>

3.71. Section 109(2) of the Law of Property Act 1925 states that a receiver "*shall be deemed to be the agent of the mortgagor; and the mortgagor shall be solely responsible for the receiver's acts or default unless the mortgage deed otherwise provides*".

3.72. Receivers are agents of the borrower, not agents of the appointing lender, so the lender will not be liable for the acts or omissions of the receivers.[80] The nature of the agency relationship has been described as "*not a true agency, but merely a formula for making the [borrower] rather than the [lender] liable for [the receivers'] acts*"[81]. Further, "*the agency of the*

---

[79] *Silven Properties Limited v Royal Bank of Scotland* [2003] EWCA Civ 1409, para 29

[80] *Ahmad v Bank of Scotland* [2016] EWCA Civ 602

[81] *Silven Properties Limited v Royal Bank of Scotland* [2003] EWCA Civ 1409 at para 26

receivers is in the nature of a device to restrict liability, not a genuine agency to assist the mortgagor".[82]

3.73. Fixed charge receivers will typically find analogous provisions in the mortgage conditions and the appointment document, and the extent of such provisions will be strictly construed.

3.74. The nature of the agency relationship has some unique characteristics that set it aside from a common law principal/agent relationship. In particular:

- The principal (i.e. the borrower) has no say in the appointment or identity of the receivers
- The borrower is not entitled to dismiss the receivers
- The borrower is not entitled to direct or provide instructions to the receivers
- The borrower has no unrestricted right of access to receivership documents or information[83]
- The receiver owes a primary duty, not to the principal, but to the lender. Only secondary duties are owed to the borrower[84]

---

82 *Menon v Pask* [2019] EWHC 2611 (Ch) para 41, relying on *Gaskell v Gosling* [1896] 1 QB 669

83 See Gomba Holdings UK Ltd v Homan [1986] 3 All ER 94 at para 100 the company borrower's "*right to information beyond the statutory accounts must in my judgment depend on demonstrating a 'need to know' for the purpose of enabling the board to exercise its residual rights or perform its duties*"

84 See Chapter 4 regarding Duties

- The receiver must manage the secured property not for the benefit of the borrower, but for the benefit of the lender to pay down and ultimately discharge the mortgage debt

- The receiver does not owe the usual common law or equitable fiduciary duties usually imposed on agents

- The receiver is entitled to remuneration via income from the mortgaged property

- The agency will continue despite the death, dissolution or insolvency of the borrower.

3.75. The effect of the receiver acting as agent for the borrower is that the receivers may take action, including the creation of legal relationships or exercise of legal and contractual powers, on behalf of the borrower without exposing themselves to personal liability. Their actions bind the borrower and liability for those actions will sit with the borrower, not the receivers. This is despite the borrower being unaware of, or even expressly not consenting to, the actions the receivers undertake as agents.

3.76. The appointment of receivers serves to displace, or paralyse, any powers the borrower had to deal with or manage the secured property.[85]

Termination of the Borrower's Agency

3.77. An overarching principle perhaps unique to receivership is that the agency relationship between borrower as principal and receiver as agent may end, together of course with the receivers'

---

85 See *Newhart Developments Ltd v Co-operative Commercial Bank Ltd [1978] QB 814* and *Moss Steamship Co. Ltd. v. Whinney [1912] A.C. 254*

power to act as agent for the borrower, but this does not bring the receivership to an end. The receivership will continue despite the absence of the agency relationship with the receivers acting on their own behalf by virtue of their appointment.

3.78. We shall consider some common circumstances in which the borrower/receiver agency relationship may end, but the receivership will survive, and the receivers can therefore continue to exercise their powers.

3.79. In relation to an individual borrower, the agency relationship enjoyed by receivers under the Law of Property Act will pass to the borrower's successors in title.[86] The agency relationship enjoyed by receivers will also pass to successors in title if the mortgage conditions make this provision. In these circumstances, on the death of the borrower the receivership will continue and the borrower's successor in title will become the principal in the continuing agency relationship.

3.80. Similarly, when an individual borrower is declared bankrupt, an existing receivership will continue. It is unclear whether the borrower's position as principal to the receivers' agency will pass to a trustee in bankruptcy.[87]

3.81. In relation to a corporate borrower, the making of a winding up order[88] will not end the receivership but if the borrower is

---

86 Section 205(1)(xvi) of the Law of Property Act 1925 which states "*"mortgagor" includes any person from time to time deriving title under the original mortgagor or entitled to redeem a mortgage according to his estate interest or right in the mortgaged property*"

87 See Part IX and Schedule 5 of the Insolvency Act 1986 with regard to the powers and function of a trustee in bankruptcy

88 And likely a Company Voluntary Arrangement under Part 1 of the Insolvency Act 1986, although there is a lack of case law

subject to a winding up order or put into liquidation, that will sever the receivers' power to act as agent of the borrower.[89] The receivers will still have their powers to deal with and sell the mortgaged property because the mortgage (and powers granted therein) will still subsist, such as the power of attorney to conduct any sale. Otherwise, the receivers will need to act in their own right.

3.82. Similarly, when a corporate borrower enters administration,[90] an existing receivership will continue. It is unclear whether the receivers will lose the power to act as the borrower's agent or the effect of the administrator's other powers in that regard.[91] It is also unclear whether the agency-principal role of the borrower passes to the Crown when a dissolved company's mortgaged property passes *bona vacantia*, although it is clear that dissolution does not end the receivership.[92]

Agent of the Lender

3.83. There are circumstances in which the receivers may act as agent for the lender, and not agent for the borrower. These circumstances may arise by accident or by design.

3.84. The lender and receivers may expressly agree that the receiver can act as the lender's agent. This may be in the terms of the mortgage agreement or in the appointment document or by way of subsequent agreement. Exercise of such powers is usually rare in practice because an agency relationship between

89 *Sowman & Others v David Samuel Trust Ltd (In Liquidation)* [1978] 1 WLR 22 and *Gosling v Gaskell and Grocott* [1897] A.C. 575

90 Under Part 2 of the Insolvency Act 1986

91 For example, the powers under paragraph 41 and 64, Schedule B1 of the Insolvency Act 1986

92 See Chapter 8 regarding termination

lender as principal and receivers as agents can lead to liability for the lender, which defeats one of the fundamental reasons for a lender to appoint receivers. However, if the agency between the borrower and the receivers is severed and receivers do not wish to act on their own behalf, they may seek to act as agents for the lender.

3.85. A lender / receiver agency relationship may arise inadvertently where the lender interferes with, or directs, the receivers.

3.86. The Court of Appeal has held that the lender "*is not responsible for what the receiver does except in so far as it gives him directions or interferes with his conduct of the realisation. If it does so, then it too is under a duty to use reasonable care.*" Further, "*Apart from intervention in the conduct of receivership, the bank can rely upon the provisions of the debenture making the receiver the agent of the company. But, it is said, if the bank gave directions to the receiver as to the conduct of the sale, the receiver became the agent of the bank; and, it is said, in such an event, if the receiver was negligent, the bank was liable.*"[93]

3.87. In *American Express v Hurley* the Court found that "*There was constant communication between the bank and the receiver and the latter sought the former's approval to such actions as he proposed to take*". In that case the borrower company went into liquidation and a short time after that, by virtue of the acts of the lender and the receiver "th*e receiver became the agent of the bank*".[94] The phrase "*directs or interferes with the receiver's activities*" is also used to describe the conduct that is necessary to inadvertently create an agency relationship between lender

93 *Standard Chartered Bank Ltd. v Walker and Another* [1982] 1 W.L.R. 1410

94 *American Express International Banking Corp. v Hurley* (1986) 2 B.C.C. 98993

and receiver, regardless of whether the original borrower/receiver agency has been severed.

3.88. In practice, it is common for receivers to consult with the appointing lender as to the progress of the receivership and key decisions on strategy and what action to take. Practitioners acting for lenders should, therefore, advise lenders to be circumspect in giving directions to receivers or following any course of action or communication which could be seen as "interfering" with or "directing" the receivers.

Summary

3.89. Receivers appointed under the Law of Property Act 1925 have a limited set of powers, but this includes a statutory power to act as agent for the borrower, thereby absolving the lender and the receivers from liability.

3.90. Receivers appointed under a fixed legal charge will typically have a wider array of contractual powers, including a power to act as agent of the borrower. They may also enjoy a power to exercise rights of the lender as donee of powers from the lender. The receivers may take on onerous liabilities for employment contracts, depending on the nature and terms of the appointment.

3.91. Receivers and lenders must be cautious that their conduct does not bring about circumstances under which the receivers act as agent for the lender. Conduct which amounts to interfering with, or directing, the receivers may be found to be acting as agents of the lender. This may create liability for the lender.

CHAPTER FOUR

DUTIES

4. Introduction

4.1. There is no statutory formulation as to the extent of receivers' duties and to whom they are owed. Nor has case law yet provided a clear and encompassing summary of the duties of a receiver. Often the case law helps to define the parameters of receiver duties by explaining what circumstances or occurrences do not amount to a breach of duty.

4.2. There are, however, a number of cases which consider receiver duties by which one can begin to construct a summary. The aim of this Chapter is to provide a brief summary of core receivership duties, rather than a detailed analysis of the wide variety of circumstances and challenges that is dealt with in the case law.

Primary Fiduciary Duty to Lender

4.3. The nature of the special relationship between the receivers, the lender and the borrower arising under the terms of the mortgage and the receivers' appointment, gives rise to a fiduciary duty of care. This duty is assumed by the receivers on acceptance of their appointment and is owed to the lender, the borrower and any other third parties interested in the equity of redemption (see further below).

4.4. However, the receivers' "*primary duty is owed to the mortgagee. His primary duty in exercising his powers is to try and bring about a situation in which the secured debt is repaid...his primary duty is to deal with and realise the security in the best interests of the mortgagee (and in particular to try to bring about a situation in which the secured debt can be and is repaid)*".[95]

4.5. The receivers' principal duty is therefore owed to the lender and it is to bring about the redemption of the mortgage debt.

4.6. In discharging this primary duty, the receivers have wider and ancillary management duties in relation to the secured property and a duty to "*be active in the protection and preservation of the charged property*".[96] They cannot, therefore, merely remain passive. This does not amount to a duty to obtain possession

Secondary Duty to Borrower

4.7. Receivers owe "*only a secondary duty to the mortgagor to exercise care to avoid preventable loss. As such,* [they] *will only be required to protect the interests of the …mortgagor where means are available, and may be given effect to, consistently with the performance of* [their] *primary duty.*"[97]

4.8. Despite this secondary duty to the borrower, receivers also owe "*a duty in exercising his powers to do so in good faith and for a proper purpose, that is to say, for the purpose of realising the assets comprising the security and obtaining repayment of the sum secured. In this regard, breach of the duty of good faith involves something more than negligence or even gross negligence: it*

---

95 *Ahmad v Bank of Scotland* [2016] EWCA Civ 602, para 38(iii)

96 *Silven Properties Limited v Royal Bank of Scotland* [2003] EWCA Civ 1409, para 23; para 27 and *Gomba Holdings v. Homan* [1986] 1 WLR 1301 para 1305

97 *Ahmad v Bank of Scotland* [2016] EWCA Civ 602 para 38

requires some dishonesty, or improper motive or element of bad faith to be established."[98]

4.9. There is no duty owed in tort by the receiver to the mortgagor, nor is there a contractual relationship between the two; the relationship is equitable. And the receiver does owe equitable duties to the borrower (as well as the lender).[99]

Duty to third parties – equity of redemption

4.10. The Court has held that receivers "*by accepting office as receivers of the properties ...assumed a fiduciary duty of care to the Bank, the Claimants and all (if any) others interested in the equity of redemption.*"[100]

4.11. It has been stated that "*the duty owed by the receiver (like the duty owed by a mortgagee) to the mortgagor is not owed to him individually but to him as one of the persons interested in the equity of redemption. The class character of the right is reflected in the class character of the relief to be granted in case of a breach of this duty. That relief is an order that the receiver account to the persons interested in the equity of redemption for what he would have held as receiver but for his default*".[101] This includes subsequent charge holders and guarantors of the mortgage.[102]

---

98 *Ahmad v Bank of Scotland* [2016] EWCA Civ 602 para 38

99 *Ahmad v Bank of Scotland* [2016] EWCA Civ 602; para 38

100 *Silven Properties Limited v Royal Bank of Scotland* [2003] EWCA Civ 1409, para 29

101 *Silven Properties Limited v Royal Bank of Scotland* [2003] EWCA Civ 1409, para 27

102 *Standard Chartered Bank v. Walker* [1982] 3 All ER 938, [1982] 1 WLR 1410

Duty of Good Faith

4.12. This includes an implied duty to act in good faith.[103] In *Medforth* it was stated that "*The extent and scope of any duty additional to that of good faith will depend on the facts and circumstances of the particular case…the breach of a duty of good faith should, in this area as in all others, require some dishonesty or improper motive, some element of bad faith, to be established.*"[104]

4.13. Dishonesty is not, however, a pre-requisite or essential component for breaching the duty of good faith.[105]

Duties concerning the secured property

4.14. There is no general duty on receivers to exercise the power of sale.[106]

4.15. With regard to the sale of the secured property, receivers are under a duty "*to take reasonable care to obtain the best price that the circumstances permit*"[107] and "*take reasonable care to obtain the true value of the property at the moment he chooses to sell it*"[108] There are limits as to what is "reasonable".

---

103 *Medforth v Blake* [2000] Ch 86

104 *Medforth v Blake* [2000] Ch 86, para 103(B)

105 *Horn v Commercial Acceptances Limited* [2011] EWHC 1757 (Ch)

106 *Routestone Ltd v. Minories Finance Ltd* [1997] BCC 180 at para 187G

107 *Standard Chartered Bank v. Walker* [1982] 3 All ER 938, [1982] 1 WLR 1410

108 *Cuckmere Brick Co Ltd and another v Mutual Finance Lt*d [1971] 2 All ER 633

4.16. This does not extend to a requirement to complete pre-marketing steps or proceed with planning applications; the receivers can discharge their duties by proceeding to an immediate sale.[109]

4.17. Receivers are not obliged to spend money on repairs prior to a sale,[110] or to carry out cosmetic work to make the property more attractive before marketing.[111]

4.18. In relation to the identity of the purchaser, the receivers cannot purchase the property as that would be a conflict of interest, as would be the case with the lender. However, "*the receiver in a case where the sale is to an associate of the appointor does not have a conflict of duty and interest as such.*"[112]

Other Issues

4.19. Receivers do not have a duty to undertake VAT accounting on behalf of the borrower and the receivers are not the taxable entity or person for the purposes of VAT. This is the case even if the powers in the mortgage are sufficient to give the receiver control over the borrower's VAT returns. There are, however, VAT considerations that receivers must be aware of. HM Revenue & Customs has published guidance on the status of receivers and practical considerations they may face regarding

109 *Silven Properties Limited v Royal Bank of Scotland* [2003] EWCA Civ 1409, para 29

110 *Meftah v. Lloyds TSB Bank* [2001] 2 All ER (Comm), paras 741 at 744 and 766

111 *Garland v. Ralph Pay & Ransom* [1984] 2 EGLR 147, para 151

112 *Devon Commercial Property Ltd v Barnett & Anor* [2019] EWHC 700 (Ch), para 194

VAT accounting and recovery of VAT on expenditure on property sales and costs.[113]

Summary

4.20. Although there is no clear and exhaustive summary of receivers' duties in either case law or statute, case law does provide guidance as to how the courts have determined the extent of receiver duties.

4.21. We have seen that core duties include: an overarching duty to the lender to take proactive steps to pay down the debt or redeem it in full. There are secondary duties to the borrower, and to others with an interest in the equity of redemption along with a duty to act in good faith.

4.22. With regard to the property, there is no duty to sell it, but if a sale is determined by the receivers to be appropriate, they must take steps to achieve the best price reasonably obtainable. They are not under a duty to improve the property, or to take any steps to add value to it; they are entitled to sell it as they find it.

[113] See HMRC Publications: "VATSC95700 – Direction of supplies: Receivers, liquidators and other insolvency practitioners: Recovery of VAT on costs incurred by mortgage lenders in respect of a sale of property under a power of sale: New arrangements" available via https://www.gov.uk/hmrc-internal-manuals/vat-supply-and-consideration/vatsc95700 and "Insolvency (VAT Notice 700/56)" available via https://www.gov.uk/guidance/insolvency-and-vat-notice-70056

CHAPTER FIVE

POSSESSION

5. Introduction

5.1. The power to take possession of the secured property is one of the key powers available to receivers. Receivers will commonly seek to take possession of the property such that it can be sold with vacant possession, thereby maximising the sale proceeds.

5.2. Receivers seeking to take possession can face a multitude of issues with regard to those in occupation, what rights they have and how they can be determined, together with the procedural requirements of service of the correct notice and pursuing a possession claim in court.

5.3. The aim of this Chapter is to provide guidance on various practical steps the receivers may consider in order to obtain possession and some common issues that are faced. The Chapter does not provide detailed guidance of the law of possession or the specifics of how to determine rights of occupation.[114]

Power to take possession

5.4. The power to take possession of the secured property is, in practical terms, significant. The power is used with the intention of either managing the property or selling it to redeem the lender's debt. The power to take possession, when exercised correctly, means that any subservient interests (e.g. a

114 Although there are some references to the Civil Procure Rules 1998 as applicable to any claim for possession undertaken in England & Wales.

tenancy) can be determined such that the property can be sold with vacant possession in order to maximise its value.

5.5. It is important to consider how the power is granted to the receivers. As above, the power to take possession is not granted by the Law of Property Act 1925. It will either by contained in the mortgage conditions or granted by the lender to the receivers in the appointment instrument.

5.6. A power granted by the mortgage conditions must be construed in accordance with its terms. It is usual for the receivers to act as deemed agent for the borrower and to enter into possession on this basis. Mortgage conditions may also enable the receivers to act as agent for the lender when entering into possession or exercising other powers.[115]

5.7. If the power to take possession is only granted or donated by the lender to the receivers in the appointment document, the receivers will act as the lender's agent and if physical possession of the property is obtained, it will be as agent for the lender, so care must be taken.

5.8. In practical terms, the receivers must ascertain who is in occupation of the property and on what basis. An assessment will need to be made as to whether the borrower has the power to determine the occupier's interest or occupation. If that can be achieved, then the receivers may exercise the power to take possession as deemed agent for the borrower. This will usually be the case for tenants or occupiers whose interest has been granted by the borrower.

5.9. The position can be more complicated when the borrower does not have a clear right to determine the occupier's interest or recover possession from him. For example, this may occur

[115] See Chapter 3 regarding powers

where the interest of the occupier takes priority over the interest of the borrower, such as an occupier with a lifetime or other beneficial interest. In those cases, it is necessary to consider whether the lender has a right to possession against the occupier and then whether the receiver can exercise the lender's powers.

5.10. There are some instances where neither the borrower nor the lender have the right to determine the interests of the occupier. The interests may take priority to the lender's and borrower's rights, or may have been expressly created so as to bind both the borrower and the lender. In such cases, the receiver will not be able to determine the interest absent agreement with the occupier.

Trespassers and unauthorised occupiers

5.11. The receivers can take action to recover the property from trespassers, i.e. occupiers who have been granted no right to occupy the property subject to the usual limited statutory protections for occupiers of this nature.[116]

5.12. An issue that can arise in practice is when neither the borrower nor the occupier are prepared to co-operate with the receivers. There may be a complete refusal to provide any information as to the right to occupation and, the terms of any tenancy or licence. In such circumstances, receivers should be advised to take reasonable steps to engage with the occupier directly, by visiting the property as well as through correspondence. If no constructive communication can be generated, the receivers may be left with the sole option of treating the occupier as a

116 See sections 3 and 5 of the Protection from Eviction Act 1977

trespasser and issuing notices and possession proceedings as agent of the borrower, based on trespass.

5.13. Provided that the correct procedural requirements for service of notice and service of the proceedings have been complied with,[117] and if the occupier declines to respond to the claim or attend the hearing, the court is likely to grant an order for possession.

5.14. The receivers should provide evidence to the court of all of the attempts made to engage with the borrower and the occupier to ascertain any rights to occupation. This is to mitigate against the risks posed by a borrower who can evidence a right to occupation after a trespass claim has been served.

5.15. If the occupier belatedly engages with the proceedings to provide evidence as to their right to occupation, the court will be unlikely to order possession based on trespass, at least at a first hearing. A failure by the occupier to prove his right to occupation prior to the issue of a trespass claim or any hearing, does not invalidate any such right. In such circumstances, it may be necessary to seek an adjournment of the possession hearing so that the receivers are afforded time to consider the right to occupation and decide whether a trespass claim is well founded, or whether the claim needs to be discontinued or amended.

Possession procedure

Types of occupier

5.16. The practical steps to exercise the power to take possession include making enquiries with the borrower and the occupier

---

117 See Rule 55.6 of the Civil Procedure Rules 1998

to ascertain who is in occupation and on what basis and obtain copies of any leases or tenancy agreements.[118]

5.17. As previously noted, shortly after appointment, receivers will usually write to occupiers to notify them of their appointment and request information. If such information is not forthcoming, receivers should conduct physical visits to the property either themselves or by contracting professional field agents.

5.18. The terms of the lease or tenancy agreement will then need to be considered to first ascertain whether the interest binds the borrower or the lender and whether the right to occupation is accepted be the receivers or not, and secondly, how that interest can be determined.

5.19. An interest that pre-dates the legal charge will bind the lender, unless it has been agreed by the parties that the occupation interest will be subject to the legal charge. A pre-dating interest that binds the lender is not one that can be determined by the lender unless the owner of the interest impliedly consented to the mortgage or the lender can rely on subrogation.[119]

5.20. An occupation interest granted by the borrower to the occupier that post-dates or is contemporaneous with the mortgage, but pre-dates the receivership appointment, is likely to be the most common scenario and the one the receivers will expect to be faced with.

---

118 See paragraph 2.52 regarding post-appointment tasks such as enquiries as to occupation

119 For example, under the Brocklesby Principle arising from *George Jobson Brocklesby v Temperance Permanent Building Society and others* [1895] AC 173

5.21. Other common scenarios include the occupation interest not being created by the borrower, such that it amounts to a trespass, and the occupation interest being created by the borrower but after the receivers were appointed.

5.22. In the former, the receivers would generally seek to take action to recover possession based on trespass in accordance with CPR Rule 55 (noting the additional requirements for claims against trespassers in Rule 55.6).

5.23. The latter is a more challenging position. Receivers can elect to consent to the right to occupation. If they do not wish to do so, they can pursue trespass action. They should also consider action against the borrower for injunctive relief to restrain the borrower granting further tenancies during the receivership.

5.24. When seeking possession, Receivers may be able to take action exercising agency powers or in their own right. Considering each in turn:

5.25. Acting as agent for the borrower – often the preferred option is for receivers to exercise powers of the borrower as the borrower's agent. Such powers to act as the borrower's agent must be expressly provided in the mortgage conditions in the case of a fixed charge receivership. In a Law of Property Act receivership, the agency powers are provided by section 109(2):

> *109(2) A receiver appointed under the powers conferred by this Act, or any enactment replaced by this Act, shall be deemed to be the agent of the mortgagor; and the mortgagor shall be solely responsible for the receiver's acts or defaults unless the mortgage deed otherwise provides.*

5.26. It is usually preferential to seek possession by exercising the borrower's agency powers due to the borrower being responsible for the acts or default of the receivers.

5.27. Any court proceedings undertaken by receivers in exercise of the borrower's right to possession, should name the claimant as the borrower acting by the receivers, and noting whether they are fixed charge receivers or Law of Property Act receivers.[120]

5.28. Absent an obligation in the mortgage conditions, the receivers are under no obligation to notify the borrower in relation to possession action that they may take. Depending on the nature of the relationships, the receivers may voluntarily provide the borrower with information and updates as to possession action, but it is more common in practice for the receivers not to do so. It is not uncommon for borrowers to have difficulty understanding the ability of receivers to take possession and to be able to commence proceedings in the borrower's own name. In circumstances where a borrower is interested in, or concerned about, the action the receivers are undertaking, receivers will be well advised to communicate clearly with borrowers in writing as to the extent of their powers and, if necessary, the consequences the borrower may face if action is taken to frustrate or interfere with the receivers' exercise of their duties.

5.29. It may be necessary for the receivers to communicate with the borrower to obtain information about occupiers, or copies of documents needed by receivers in order to take possession action, such as the tenancy agreement, tenancy deposit information, gas safety records and energy performance

120 By way of illustration, the claimant may be described as the borrower acting by the receivers: "Mr John Smith acting by Clare Brown and Paul Gray (Joint Fixed Charge Receivers)"

certificates. If such information is essential and not forthcoming, the receivers can make an application for pre-action disclosure under against the borrower and, or in the alternative, the tenant/occupier.[121]

5.30. In some circumstances receivers may need to exercise the lender's rights. It may be the case that the tenancy, or other interests, bind the borrower but not the lender, for example, if an occupier's tenancy binds the borrower and cannot be terminated by the borrower (or by receivers exercising the borrower's agency powers) but post-dates the lender's charge so does not bind the lender.

5.31. Careful consideration must be given as to whether it is appropriate for the receivers to exercise the lender's powers, or whether it is preferential in the circumstances for the lender to take its own action directly and terminate the receivers' appointment.

5.32. The receivers can only exercise the lender's rights if the lender's rights are delegated to them by the mortgage conditions or some other instrument. In this instance, the receivers will be named individually as the claimants.[122]

Borrower in occupation

5.33. It is not uncommon for individual borrowers to go into occupation of the secured property, despite it being usually a condition of their buy-to-let mortgage that they must not do so or are only permitted to let the property to suitable tenants.

---

121 See Rule 31.16 of the Civil Procedure Rules 1998

122 This is because the receivers are acting as donees of a power given to them by the lender, rather than acting as agent of the borrower.

5.34. There is both conceptual and practical difficulty in receivers, acting as agent of the borrower, seeking possession from the borrower.

5.35. There may be the ability for receivers to exercise powers granted or donated by the lender.[123] A High Court decision has provided clarity on how receivers can proceed when faced with this situation: receivers with a power to take possession and a power of sale can exercise these powers by seeking possession from a borrower in occupation. Possession must be sought by the receivers acting in their own name, rather than as agent for the borrower.[124]

5.36. In these circumstances, the borrower has the right to make proposals to redeem the mortgage debt and the right to seek an adjournment, stay or suspension of any order pursuant to section 36 of the Administration of Justice Act 1970 because receivers derive title under the mortgagee for the purposes of section 39(1).[125]

Management agents or sub-tenants

5.37. It is not uncommon for borrowers to have granted contractual rights to third parties to create or manage sub-tenants or occupiers. These range from informal, unwritten arrangements between family members, to more formal commercial agreements for the appointment of a management agent with a right to grant tenancies, either in their own name

123 See paragraphs 3.70 regarding agency powers

124 *Menon v Pask* [2019] EWHC 2611 (Ch)

125 *Menon v Pask* [2019] EWHC 2611 (Ch) para 43

or in the name of the borrower or formal leases which permit sub-letting.

5.38. Receivers will need to understand the role of each party and seek to obtain copies of all contractual documentation. This will likely involve communication with all relevant parties to explain the receivers' appointment, powers and duties and make formal written requests for information and documentation concerning their position. This may include leases, sub-leases, management agreements or licence agreements.

5.39. Receivers will need to decide whether it is necessary to determine the interests of such third parties. Interests that amount to an estate in land, for example leases, will need to be terminated in accordance with their terms and any applicable statutory procedures such as those contained in the Housing Acts.

5.40. Where the relationship does not amount to an estate in land, such as commercial management agreements, the receivers will need to determine whether they have the power to terminate the agreement exercising the powers of the borrower. Whether or not the receivers have this power will depend on the extent of powers set out in the mortgage conditions. In the case of receivers appointed solely under the Law of Property Act, there are no express powers to terminate commercial contracts.

5.41. If the receivers do have the power to terminate contracts, then they can terminate such agreements. Any liability under such contract, or liability for damages for breach of contract, is a liability of the borrower and not the receivers, provided they have acted in accordance with their powers.

Equitable interests

5.42. Receivers may find themselves appointed over a secured property which is subject to equitable interests. Third parties asserting rights of occupation pursuant to equitable rights must be handled with particular care.

5.43. Equitable interests may arise where the borrower is the legal owner and registered as the proprietor of the secured property at HM Land Registry, but where the beneficial ownership sits with a third party. In other words, the borrower may hold the property on trust for someone else.

5.44. Express trusts may be registered at HM Land Registry and ascertainable from a review of the proprietorship register. They may also be within the knowledge of the lender or have been entered into with the lender's consent.

5.45. However, constructive trusts will not, by their very nature, be registered at HM Land Registry and are unlikely to have been consented to by the lender.

5.46. The existence of a trust will not necessarily prevent the receivers from continuing to discharge their duties and obtain possession but much will depend on the nature of the trust, whether the equitable interests amount to a right to occupy, and when the trust was created.

5.47. Generally, an equitable interest binding on the borrower will also likely be binding on the receivers acting solely as agents for the borrower.

5.48. The following approach is recommended:

5.49. Firstly, consider whether or not the beneficiary of the trust has a right to occupy the property. If not, then the receiver may be able to seek possession as agent of the borrower. However, if the beneficiary does have a right to occupation, then it may be necessary to consider other options.

5.50. Secondly, consider whether the trust binds the lender. For example, where the beneficiary's equitable interest and actual occupation pre-dates the lender's charge, the interest is likely to bind the lender. There may be exceptions, such as where his interest was declared to the lender and he agreed to subject his interest to that of the lender, or under Schedule 3, paragraph 2 to the Land Registration Act 2002. Where a trust binds a lender, the lender (and receivers exercising the lender's right to sale) will likely not be entitled to possession and therefore will only be able to sell the property subject to the beneficiary's interest/occupation.

5.51. An equitable interest will likely not bind a lender where it post-dates the lender's charge or is otherwise expressly subject to the lender's charge.

5.52. If an equitable interest does not bind a lender, then receivers may be able to exercise the lender's powers and rights, such as the power to take possession and the power of sale. However, these powers must be delegated to the receivers in the mortgage conditions or appointment document. It is, therefore, necessary to carefully consider the terms of the mortgage and appointment to understand the extent of such delegation.

5.53. If the necessary powers are not delegated to the receivers in the mortgage conditions or appointment document, then the lender may be able to delegate such powers to the receivers in a separate, post-appointment instrument. In that case, the receivers will not be acting in such action as the agent of the borrower, but as a donee or delegate of the lender's powers.

5.54. The alternative is for the receivers' appointment to be terminated and for the lender to pursue its own remedies on the basis that the lender has the stronger claim to possession.

5.55. A further option to consider when receivers are dealing with equitable interest, is whether a commercial settlement can be achieved with the beneficiary. In practice, beneficiaries with a right to occupation may be willing to "buy out" the lender or surrender their interests.

Settlement

5.56. Any occupier or person claiming another interest in the property may determine that interest by way of commercial settlement between the parties. Such settlement may occur at the pre-action stage, or after proceedings are underway. Any settlement should be properly documented in the usual way, for example, by settlement agreement or deed or by way of consent or Tomlin order if proceedings are underway.

5.57. If the settlement includes a determination of an occupier's interest, care will need to be given as to whether a deed of surrender is required and whether the receivers have the power to accept surrenders and the formalities of a surrender of a tenancy.[126]

5.58. Receivers should consider how a settlement could advance their strategy for the property on a commercial basis. This may include rent free periods, ex gratia payments in exchange for vacant possession being provided or payment of legal or other costs incurred by the tenant/occupier. Such payments may be considered an expense of the receivership and should be invoiced to the lender, although receivers should beware of

126 See paragraph 3.33 regarding surrenders

unreasonably generous payments being open to challenge by the borrower.

Acting for lenders when receivers seek possession

5.59. Lenders will typically expect receivers to undertake possession action acting as the agent for the borrower or in their own right. Such action does not involve the lender, who is effectively insulated from it and any liability so arising, for example, from adverse cost orders in possession litigation.

5.60. If receivers wish to exercise the rights of the lender, the lender should assess whether the receivers have the power delegated to them in the mortgage conditions or a separate instrument and whether it may be beneficial for the lender to take the action directly. For example, it may be less costly for the lender to take direct action. Consideration should also be made as to whether it is beneficial to terminate the receivership or if there are reasons for the receivers to remain appointed, whilst the lender takes possession action, for example, to collect rent.

5.61. Lenders may be approached by receivers who are proposing a commercial settlement in order to obtain vacant possession and determine the interest of an occupier. Such settlement may amount to surrenders of tenancies, and payment of legal or other costs, or ex gratia payments to occupiers. Such sums are expenses of the receivership and can be invoiced to the lender. In practice, receivers are likely to approach lenders to explain their intentions and provide the lender with an opportunity to consent or object. Lenders will need to ensure that such costs or payments can correctly be debited to the mortgage account.

Position of Borrower

5.62. Borrowers should ascertain the basis on which the receivers are acting i.e. exercising the rights of the borrower or the lender, arising from the mortgage conditions or the Law of Property Act 1925 and the specific extent of those powers.

5.63. If the receivers are acting outside of the scope of their powers, or in breach of their duties, the borrower has an ability to apply for injunctive relief against the receivers and further or alternatively, sue the receivers for damages.[127]

5.64. The correct way to do so would be a separate claim by the borrower against the receivers. Alternatively, if the receivers have commenced litigation to gain possession, borrowers can make an application to be added as a party under CPR Rule 19.4.

5.65. Receivers may contact borrowers and try to obtain information about occupiers, or copies of documents needed by receivers in order to take possession action, such as the tenancy agreement or lease, tenancy or rent deposit information, gas safety records and energy performance certificates.

5.66. Borrowers faced with such requests should first investigate what, if any, obligations exist under the mortgage conditions to provide such information to the receivers. Secondly, borrowers should consider whether they wish to support the receivers in discharging their duties and obtaining possession. Assisting the receivers may minimise receivership costs, which may be in the interests of the borrower. However, in more contentious situations this will not be feasible.

---

127 See Chapter 3 regard receiver powers and Chapter 4 regarding duties

Occupiers

5.67. Occupiers or tenants should firstly ascertain the basis on which the occupier is occupying the property, obtain copies of any leases or tenancy agreements and ancillary contractual or statutory documentation regarding the occupier's interests.

5.68. Secondly, they should ascertain the basis on which the receivers are acting i.e. exercising the rights of the borrower or the lender, arising from the mortgage conditions or the Law of Property Act 1925 and the specific extent of those powers and the receivers' strategy. For example, whether it is to obtain vacant possession and sell the property or otherwise and also whether the receivers accept the occupier's right to occupation or whether they deny it, which will likely depend on when the occupier's rights of occupation were created and by whom.

5.69. There may be scope for negotiation as to the duration of the continued occupation and surrender of the tenancy, with an agreed date to hand possession to the receivers without the need for litigation and the costs liability associated with litigation. Such negotiation should ideally take place at a pre-action stage but can also take place after the issue of possession proceedings and be documented by way of a consent or Tomlin order which may, depending on the wording, amount to a possession order which can be capable of enforcement by warrant for possession or writ of possession under CPR 83 in the usual way.

5.70. Receivers may be willing to negotiate other commercial terms, such as a payment of legal costs incurred by the occupier or even payment of an ex gratia sum to accept a surrender.

5.71. If the receivers are acting outside of the scope of their powers, or in breach of their duties, tenants could seek appropriate injunctive or declaratory relief in proceedings against the receivers and, or in the alternative, damages. This may be by way of separate proceedings, or as a Part 20 claim within proceedings brought by the receivers.

Summary

5.72. This chapter has considered various practical steps that receivers can take in order to ascertain who is in possession. It considers the receivers' power to take possession and how that can be exercised regarding various classes of occupier, such as trespassers, tenants, sub-tenants and people with a beneficial interest, as well as the role of managing agents.

5.73. Settlement should be considered at all times and receivers should be aware that litigation to obtain a possession order may be necessary but there may also be scope for agreeing terms for the surrender of possession, which can save considerable time and costs if litigation can be avoided.

CHAPTER SIX

SALE

6. Introduction

6.1. A power of sale is granted to mortgage lenders, but not to receivers, under the Law of Property Act 1925. This absence of a statutory power of sale for receivers is significant.

6.2. A power of sale must be granted to the receiver in the mortgage conditions. It is therefore essential to carefully consider the mortgage conditions to understand if a power of sale is granted to receivers and, if so, the extent of that power.

6.3. Commonly the power is either granted directly to the receivers in the mortgage conditions or expressly granted to the lender and then donated or delegated to the receivers.

6.4. The aim of this chapter is to provide some practical guidance on the sales process in receivership cases and key differences or nuances that may apply to receivers. This chapter does not aim to provide detailed guidance on the conveyancing procedure.

Pre-sale considerations

6.5. Receivers are not under an obligation or duty to sell the secured property. Their overriding duty is to arrange for the mortgage debt to be redeemed.[128] In practice, the power of sale is commonly exercised to sell the secured property such that the sale proceeds can be used to redeem the mortgage debt.

---

128 See Chapter 4 regarding duties

6.6. If the receivers are pursuing a sale strategy, they can either market and sell the property themselves once they have vacant possession or, alternatively, they may decide to sell the property subject to the existing rights of occupation. Or they may hand possession to the lender so that the lender can arrange a sale as mortgagee in possession.

6.7. In practice, receivers will need to obtain an up-to-date mortgage balance from the lender and conduct market appraisals to ascertain the range of likely selling prices for the property and whether the price will redeem the mortgage. Other considerations should include:

- Whether the property is tenanted and, if so, on what terms and whether obtaining vacant possession is preferrable to maximise the sale price

- Professional valuations should be obtained so the receivers can satisfy themselves as to the value of the property – receivers should consider whether a number of valuations should be obtained and the basis on which the valuations are prepared[129]

- An appropriate marketing strategy

- Method of sale – auction or private treaty

[129] For example, will simple sale appraisals suffice, or are more details valuations required, for example under RICS "Red Book" guidelines. Factors which are relevant to this assessment are the likely value of the property, the secured debt, any projected surplus or shortfall and other associated risks.

- The timing of the sale (note that there is no duty to delay a sale in the expectation that the value may increase, for example, where market values are increasing)

- The Receivers are under no duty to improve the property or take steps to increase value, such as carry out repair work, seek planning permission or complete the grant of leases – they can sell the property as they find it[130]

- A sale to an associate of the receiver or the lender will carry increased risks and may come under scrutiny, including consideration as to whether the sale was for an improper purpose

- Fair and reasonable consideration should be given to proposals from third parties with a special interest in the property, such as neighbours, subsequent mortgagees or family members of the borrower.

6.8. If selling the property, receivers have a duty to both the lender and the borrower to obtain the best price reasonably obtainable at the time.[131]

6.9. It is recommended that decision making and evidence considered, including professional valuation or marketing advice, should be retained by the receivers as a matter of good record keeping and to assist in a rebutting any subsequent challenges.

---

130 See Chapter 4 regarding duties including duties regarding the secured property and its sale

131 See *Silven Properties Ltd v Royal Bank of Scotland Plc* [2003] EWCA Civ 1409

6.10. If the borrower has paid or tendered the sum required to redeem the full mortgage debt, then the receivers should not proceed with a sale.[132]

6.11. If the receivers decide to exercise a power of sale. The power of sale may either empower the receivers to: (a) exercise the borrower's power of sale; or (b) exercise the lender's power of sale.

6.12. Consideration should always be given to the potential liability of receivers and how that can be mitigated. Section 37(1) Insolvency Act 1986 states that a receiver appointed over a company borrower is "*personally liable on any contract entered into by him in the performance of his functions (except insofar as the contract otherwise provides)*". It is therefore crucial to include an exclusion of liability in favour of the receivers in any contract for sale and include suitable exclusions for representations and suitable warranties.[133] Note, in particular, it is prudent not to include any warranty around vacant possession to mitigate risks associated with occupation (which receivers may have limited control over).

6.13. The timing of exchange and completion can be of great significant in receiver cases, particularly as the borrower retains a right to redeem the mortgage debt up to the point of completion.[134] For that reason, simultaneous exchange and completion is preferable in order to mitigate these risks.

---

[132] *Gomba Holdings UK Ltd v Homan* [1986] 3 All ER 94

[133] It is suggested that a contractual right for receivers to terminate the contract prior to completion is likely to be unpalatable for buyers and is not therefore commonly seen

[134] See *National Westminster Bank Plc v Hunter and Another* [2011] EWHC 3170 (Ch)

Receivers exercising Borrower's Power of Sale

6.14. In exercising the borrower's power of sale, the receiver will act as agent for the borrower and will contract in the borrower's name and, if they have the power to do so, will bind the borrower to any other terms contained in the sale contract. The receivers' sale of the property will also be subject to any interests or rights which bind the borrower, such as third-party rights of occupation granted by the borrower. In order for the receivers to sell the property free of such rights, it is common in practice for receivers to have determined any such rights and obtained vacant possession prior to any sale.

6.15. If there are other third-party interests which the borrower (and receivers exercising the borrower's power) cannot sell free of, it is prudent to explore whether a sale using the lender's power of sale is preferable.[135]

6.16. In relation to leasehold property, restrictions on alienation and consent to assign should be carefully considered. It is not uncommon, in receivership cases, for the borrower to be in debt or in dispute with freeholders or managing agents in relation to service charges, ground rent or disrepair issues. Receivers should investigate these issues in good time, prior to any sale negotiations, such that appropriate action can be taken to avoid undue delays to a sale and associated increased costs. If such issues do affect the property, receivers may wish to explore options to settle any disputes with freeholders or managing agents at an early stage.

Sale process

6.17. The form of the transfer document is the same as the borrower would utilise in a standard sale: Form TR1 or Form TP1,

[135] See paragraph 6.25 regarding the lender's power of sale

dependent on whether all or part of the registered estate is being sold.

6.18. HMLR Practice Guide 36A provides guidance on how receivers should execute the relevant form for both individual and corporate borrowers.[136]

6.19. Following redemption of the mortgage debt, a discharge (form DS1) should be filed at HM Land Registry by, or on behalf of, the lender to ensure that its charge is removed from the charges register.

6.20. As the power of sale being exercised is the borrower's, all of the usual restrictions will need to be complied with. For example, any restrictions on the title which bind the borrower, including any restriction in favour of the lender who appointed the receivers, will need to be complied with. Similarly, restrictions in favour of any subsequent lenders will also need to be complied with in the usual way, as if the borrower were selling the property.

6.21. Sale contracts often include exclusion clauses preventing any warranties concerning the authority under which the receivers act.

6.22. As with any sale by a borrower, registration of the transfer at HM Land Registry must be made using Form AP1. However,

136 https://www.gov.uk/government/publications/dispositions-executed-by-law-of-property-act-receivers/practice-guide-36a-receivers-appointed-under-the-provisions-of-the-law-of-property-act-1925

HM Land Registry impose additional requirements for receiver sales which are set out in Practice Guide 36A:[137]

If your application for registration is based on a disposition by a receiver, we will require, in addition to the normal evidence:

- *the mortgage or a certified copy of it (but not if the title is registered and the mortgage is already registered or noted and a copy is filed with us, containing all the applicable terms and conditions of the mortgage – see further below). We will check that the mortgage:*
    - *is properly executed*
    - *contains the appropriate provisions to allow the receiver to be appointed and to carry out the disposition (if these provisions are not apparent from the mortgage deed itself, or from the copy filed with us, then other evidence, such as the mortgage terms and conditions, should be lodged)*
- *has been registered under section 395 of the Companies Act 1985 or section 860, section 878 or section 859A of the Companies Act 2006, where the borrower is a company registered under the Companies Acts*
- *evidence that the power of appointment of a receiver under the mortgage has arisen. Where the receiver's appointment is made by court order, the order (or a certified copy) will suffice. Where the appointment is not made by the court we will require evidence (such as a certificate by the chargee or*

137 https://www.gov.uk/government/publications/dispositions-executed-by-law-of-property-act-receivers/practice-guide-36a-receivers-appointed-under-the-provisions-of-the-law-of-property-act-1925

by their conveyancer on their behalf) that the power of appointment under the mortgage or debenture has arisen, unless this is evident from a full copy of the mortgage or debenture filed at HM Land Registry

- *the instrument of appointment of the receiver or a certified copy of it (if joint receivers are appointed but only one has executed the transfer or lease, the appointment must state whether they can act jointly and severally)*

- *a release or discharge from all mortgages or charges, including the mortgage, from which the applicant is to take the property free. If the title is already registered, the release or discharge will need to cover only those mortgages or charges that have been protected in the register*

- *if the receiver executes as attorney, evidence of non-revocation where appropriate: see Execution by Law of Property Act receiver*

- *details of any challenge to the validity of the mortgage (for example by a third-party or a creditor (including another lender)) that is within the actual knowledge of the Law of Property Act receiver or the applicant. Where the borrower is a company and the challenge is by a liquidator or administrator of the company, or the borrower is an individual or partnership and the challenge is by a trustee in bankruptcy, details of the name and address of the liquidator, administrator or trustee in bankruptcy should be provided*

6.23. Complications may arise where the borrower's estate is held on trust.[138]

6.24. If the sale contract is executed by the receivers under a power of attorney (as distinct from execution as the borrower's agent), either contained in the mortgage conditions or granted separately, there are additional requirements on registration of the transfer at HM Land Registry which are contained In Land Registry Practice Guides 8, 9 and 36A.

Receivers' exercising the Lender's Power of Sale

6.25. Lenders enjoy a power of sale which is granted by statute under section 101 of the Law of Property Act 1925. The statutory power of sale may also be varied, restricted or extended by the mortgage conditions. In addition, lenders may delegate their power of sale to receivers so that receivers may exercise the lender's power of sale.

6.26. Exercising the lender's power of sale may be preferable where there are interests on the property title which the lender could overreach, but which may bind the borrower and receivers exercising the borrower's power of sale.

Statutory power of sale

6.27. Section 101 of the Law of Property Act 1925 provides:

101 Powers incident to estate or interest of mortgagee.

(1) A mortgagee, where the mortgage is made by deed, shall, by virtue of this Act, have the following powers, to the like extent as if they

138 See HM Land Registry Practice Guide 36A

had been in terms conferred by the mortgage deed, but not further (namely):

(i) A power, when the mortgage money has become due, to sell, or to concur with any other person in selling, the mortgaged property, or any part thereof, either subject to prior charges or not, and either together or in lots, by public auction or by private contract, subject to such conditions respecting title, or evidence of title, or other matter, as the mortgagee thinks fit, with power to vary any contract for sale, and to buy in at an auction, or to rescind any contract for sale, and to re-sell, without being answerable for any loss occasioned thereby

6.28. The requirements therefore are, firstly, that the mortgage is made by deed and, secondly, that the mortgage money has become due.

6.29. The effect of the power is that the lender can sell the whole, or part, of the borrower's freehold or leasehold property. It does not restrict the lender in selling only its own security interest. Nor does it require the lender to obtain possession of the proprietor before being sold. To put it another way, the lender is entitled to sell the property as mortgagee in possession or as mortgagee not in possession. In the latter case, the lender would expect to receive a lower sale price if it cannot deliver vacant possession to the buyer.

6.30. The exercise of the statutory power of sale is regulated by section 103 of the Law of Property Act 1925 which provides:

103 Regulation of exercise of power of sale.

A mortgagee shall not exercise the power of sale conferred by this Act unless and until—

(i) Notice requiring payment of the mortgage money has been served on the mortgagor or one of two or more mortgagors, and default has been made in payment of the mortgage money, or of part thereof, for three months after such service; or

(ii) Some interest under the mortgage is in arrear and unpaid for two months after becoming due; or

(iii) There has been a breach of some provision contained in the mortgage deed or in this Act, or in an enactment replaced by this Act, and on the part of the mortgagor, or of some person concurring in making the mortgage, to be observed or performed, other than and besides a covenant for payment of the mortgage money or interest thereon.

6.31. The lender is not restricted in the method of sale and, accordingly, sale by private treaty or auction are both permissible.

Express contractual power of sale

6.32. In modern practice, mortgage conditions will generally include an express power of sale which may be more extensive than the statutory power, or exercisable in different circumstances.

Can the Lender's power of sale be delegated to Receivers?

6.33. There is some debate over whether the lender's power of sale can be delegated to receivers. There is no express provision in the Law of Property Act delegating the lender's power of sale to receivers and the HM Land Registry Practice Guides 75 and 36A do not provide any guidance. Some sources conclude that the lender's power of sale can be delegated to receivers if the mortgage terms so provide.

Sale process

6.34. There are specific HM Land Registry forms that must be used when exercising a lender's power of sale. These are Form TR2 for the transfer of the whole of the title and Form TP1 for the transfer of part of a title.

6.35. The lender should be named as the transferor (see para 2.1 of HM Land Registry Practice guide 75: transfer under a chargee's power of sale).[139]

6.36. There are three options:

6.37. Firstly, for the lender to execute the transfer, as a direct exercise of its power of sale.

6.38. Secondly, the receivers may execute the transfer and provide evidence of their power to do so under the mortgage conditions, namely, the mortgage conditions and the appointment document.

6.39. Thirdly, the receivers execute as attorney for the lender and provide HM Land Registry with a copy of the power of attorney granting the receivers power to execute the transfer in the lender's name.

6.40. A discharge DS1 is not required where the lender's power of sale is being exercised.

---

139 https://www.gov.uk/government/publications/transfer-under-a-chargees-power-of-sale/practice-guide-75-transfer-under-a-chargees-power-of-sale

Overreaching

6.41. When the transfer under the lender's power of sale is registered at HM Land Registry, any entries on the title register that post-dated the lender's charge, will typically be cancelled and removed by the Registrar.

6.42. This only applies to entries which are registered later in time than the date of registration of the lender's charge.

6.43. If there are entries on the title which pre-date the lender's charge, these will not be removed or cancelled and will remain on the title unless separately removed by way of application.

Borrowers

6.44. Sale contracts entered into by receivers exercising the borrower's power of sale will bind the borrower and the borrower will be liable for any claims arising. This may include other terms within the sale contract, provided that the receivers have the power to do so in the mortgage terms. For example, these principles will apply to claims for specific performance of the sale contract or claims for damages for breach of contract by the purchaser.

6.45. A common area of concern for borrowers is the sale price and when the property is being undervalued. In practical terms the concern may be that the receivers will seek a quick sale at a low price, rather than pursue more extensive marketing activities so as to maximise the sale price.

6.46. If the borrower has legitimate concerns about the valuation of the property or the marketing strategy adopted by receivers, the borrower cannot make a complaint to the lender if it is a receiver sale using borrower powers. However, the borrower can seek injunctive relief against the receivers where there is evidence that the sale is at an undervalue. Careful consideration should be given to any such claim in light of the receivers' extensive powers and the extent of their duties (for example, their right to sell the property as they find it, rather than undertake works to increase value).[140]

6.47. A sale of the secured property by receivers may also be restrained if the borrower has tendered payment of the full mortgage debt and this option is available right up until completion of the receivers' sale.[141]

6.48. A further area of contention can be the storage of the borrower's goods on the property. In a sale, receivers acting as agent for the borrower, will likely be under a contractual obligation to give vacant possession and if the borrower's goods are left at property, there may be a breach of the obligation to give vacant possession which may give rise to liability against the borrower (not the receivers). Borrowers are recommended to engage with receivers in relation to retrieval and storage of goods prior to any sale completing, to avoid such liability.[142] It is sensible for receivers to advice the borrower as to the timing of exchange and completion so that issues can be identified in advance and disputes resolved.

6.49. As detailed above, on registration of the transfer the applicant (being the receivers or their conveyancer) is under an obligation to notify the Registrar of "*details of any challenge to*

---

140 See Chapter 4 regarding duties

141 See *National Westminster Bank Plc v Hunter and Another* [2011] EWHC 3170 (Ch)

142 See *Nigel Marsay & Nigel's Computer Repairs Limited v Barclays Bank UK Plc & others* [2023] EWHC 2301 (Comm) for a recent summary of the principles regarding a sale at an undervalue and chattels left on the secured property.

the validity of the mortgage (for example by a third-party or a creditor (including another lender)) that is within the actual knowledge of the Law of Property Act receiver or the applicant".[143] It follows that if the borrower has lodged any challenge to the validity of the mortgage under which the receivers are appointed, the receivers or their conveyancers should be notified of this obligation and the borrower can, in principle, also notify the Registrar.

Purchasers

6.50. As detailed above, a sale by receivers exercising the borrower's power of sale is broadly similar to a standard property sale conducted by the borrower, subject to some additional requirements.

6.51. Buyers may consider a receiver sale to come with some increased risks, particularly around the receivers' appointment, vacant possession, goods left at the property and potential challenges brought, or obstructions caused, by the borrower.

6.52. Any breaches of contract (where receivers have acted as agent for the borrower) will be breaches of the borrower (not the receivers personally) and it is suggested that some enhanced pre-completion due diligence would be prudent so as to allow time for any practical or legal complexities around the property, it contents, any third-party interests and the title, to be dealt with in good time. Such issues can cause delay to completion or registration of the transfer and increased costs.

6.53. This should include pre-contractual enquiries around the validity and registration of the legal charge under which the

143 See paragraph 7 of HM Land Registry Practice Guide 36A

receivers are appointed and the validity of the appointment of the receivers.

6.54. Buyers should take particular care to understand the contractual provisions and exclusions regarding the receivers' authority to act, the validity of the appointment, vacant possession and whether this extends to the remove of goods from the property prior to the sale. Buyers would also be well advised to carry out sufficient due diligence to ensure it is receiving a clean title, or at least any issues are identified prior to exchange and completion. It may also be prudent for buyers to require the receivers to provide the evidence which the receivers must provide to HM Land Registry. In the case of a leasehold title, restrictions on alienation and consent to assign should be carefully considered.

6.55. It is important for those advising buyers to understand that, where the receivers are exercising the borrower's power of sale, rights of overreaching enjoyed by the lender will not arise. So on sale of the property, any undischarged registered charges, interests noted on the register (such as Unilateral Notices) and rights of occupation under Schedule 3 of the Land Registration Act 2002 will remain and be subject to the sale. Any other security interests over the title being purchased should be identified and it would be prudent to require the receiver to arrange for their release prior to completion of any sale.

Proceeds of Sale

6.56. Proceeds of sale will be used to redeem the mortgage debt and must be handled in accordance with the provisions of section 105 of the Law of Property Act 1925. In simple cases, the first ranking priority lender will be entitled to recover its full debt out of the sale proceeds, before any subsequent lenders with lower ranking priority receive any payment. The usual rules on priority of discharge can be altered by intercreditor agreements. Receivers appointed by lower ranking charge holders will be particularly concerned with the priority of discharge the likelihood of available funds, once the first ranking lender's debt is redeemed. There may, of course, be insufficient funds to redeem all secured lenders.

6.57. Funds will be held by the receivers, the lender or their conveyancers and, if there is any uncertainty or dispute as to the entitled party or their whereabouts, an application can be made to pay the sums into court under section 63 of the Trustee Act 1925 and paragraph 6.1 to Practice Direction 37 of the Civil Procedure Rules 1998.

Summary

6.58. We have seen that receivers will commonly have several options as to how to proceed with a sale. These may include exercising the borrower's power of sale as agent for the borrower, or exercising the lender's power of sale, if that has been delegated to the receivers.

6.59. Where there are interests on the property title that may bind the borrower (and receivers exercise the borrower's power as agents), then exercising the lender's power of sale may be preferable, if that option is available to receivers.

6.60. There are some specific requirements regarding HM Land Registry practice that receivers exercising a borrower's power of sale must comply with.

CHAPTER SEVEN

CHALLENGES AND LITIGATION

7. Introduction

7.1. Challenges against receivers may occur at various stages of the receivership and these often result in litigation.

7.2. Common challenges include challenges around the validity or enforceability of the legal charge, invalid or defective appoints. A further area of common challenge is around the conduct of the receivers and whether they are acting lawfully in the discharge of their duties.

7.3. Challenges are commonly made by borrowers, who of course have a key interest in the receivership. Challenges may also be made by lenders, other third parties, such as occupiers of secured properties or those claiming beneficial interests.

7.4. Receivers will often need to engage in litigation, for example, to recover rent or obtain possession of the secured property, or to seek directions from the court. Receivers may also face claims brought against them by borrowers or third parties.

7.5. In this chapter, different types of common claims are considered, together with a summary of the receivers' powers to engage in litigation and other common issues that may be faced in practice. Specialist texts on litigation or civil procedure should be consulted in relation to detailed guidance and law on bringing and defending claims in the courts of England and Wales.

Challenges concerning Invalid or Defective Appointments

7.6. An invalid appointment is one which can have no legal effect, such as where the appointing lender had no power to make the appointment, or if the appointing lender did have the power to make the appointment, but where the contractual or statutory conditions were not satisfied.

7.7. An appointment will be defective where the appointing lender had the power to make the appointment, and the pre-conditions were met, but where there is a defect in making the appointment, for example, the formalities of the appointment were not complied with.

Lender

7.8. A lender aware of an invalid or defective appointment should take steps, as far as is possible, to remedy the defect and re-appoint the received on a valid basis. The remedial action will depend on the nature or cause of the defect or invalidity. There is no restriction on terminating a receiver appointment that may be defective in some way and reappointing the same receivers or alternative receivers. It is not uncommon for receivers to be appointed for a period of time, for the appointment to be terminated and then a reappointment to be made at a later date.[144]

7.9. It is conceivable that a borrower may have recourse to a lender in relation to any losses or costs he has suffered as a result of a defective or invalid appointment, subject to the usual rules around recovery of damages. The lender will not, however, be liable to the borrower or others for the acts of the receivers under a defective or invalid appointment.

144 See Chapter 8 on termination

Receiver

7.10. If receivers become aware of a defect in their appointment, they should take urgent action to address the matter. Receivers purporting to act under an invalid or defective appointment will have no right to possession of the secured property and will be committing a trespass if they enter or remain in possession and will be liable as trespassers. Similarly, the receivers will have none of the statutory powers, such as entitlement to collect income or remuneration, although they may still be able to claim remuneration from the lender under the terms of the mortgage agreement.

7.11. Receivers may also have liability to third parties to whom they have held themselves out as validly appointed receivers.

Borrower

7.12. In practice, it is not uncommon for pre-appointment negotiations between the lender and borrower to continue after an appointment has been made, particularly around proposals for redemption. However, after receivers have been appointed, any continued negotiations will likely need to involve the receivers as well as the lender. The receivers may be prepared to allow a short period of time for a redemption to take place but there is no requirement for them to do so and much will depend on the circumstances, including the value of the asset against the debt and the prevailing market conditions for the property.[145]

7.13. If the borrower has already appointed agents to market the property for sale, the receivers should be furnished with this information.

[145] See Chapter 4 regarding duties

7.14. Borrowers served with a notification that the lender has appointed receivers should satisfy themselves that the appointment is valid. It is necessary to review the facility agreement and all applicable terms and conditions and check that any relevant statutory or contractual requirements have been complied with.[146]

7.15. The course of action available will depend upon the stage of the appointment and any action undertaken by receivers. If the appointment has already been accepted, the principal step will be to challenge the appointment if it is invalid or defective. Remedies such as injunctive relief to restrain the receivers from acting under the appointment or taking steps such as demanding or collecting rent, corresponding with tenants, seeking possession and sale may, be appropriate, following the usual common law principles governing the granting of injunctive relief.

7.16. In addition, there may be grounds for declaratory relief concerning the appointment, and claims for damages against receivers acting unlawfully. For example, in relation to trespass on the secured property, interference with the contractual relationship with the tenants or other losses.[147] It is conceivable that the borrower may also explore whether any causes of action lie against the lender, for example, for damages for breach of contract if the terms of the mortgage contract were breached by the lender causing the borrower loss, or even injunctive relief if further lender action is pending. Again, the usual common law principles of recovery will be applied.

7.17. If receivers have been validly appointed, borrowers would be well advised to either cooperate with receivers or at least adopt

---

[146] See Chapter 2 regarding appointments

[147] See, for example, *OBG Ltd v Allan* [2007] 2 WLR 920

a neutral stance. This is with the intention of minimising the receivers' costs, which are likely to be added to the borrower's indebtedness, and to avoid allegations of, and potential liability caused by, obstructing the receivers' in discharging their duties. Borrowers retain, at all times, a right to redeem the secured debt. If the debt is redeemed, then the receivership will be brought to an end. Borrowers who object to the appointment of receivers may be well advised to explore options for redeeming the debt, for example, through a refinancing arrangement with a third party lender.

7.18. It is common for borrowers to seek to make a payment towards the secured debt shortly after the appointment of receivers. This is with the intention of belatedly curing the default or in the mistaken belief that the receivers will be prevented from continuing if, for example, arrears have been paid or a loan-to-value ratio breach has been cured. However, such attempts are often futile because the receivership continues until the receivers' appointment is terminated by the lender or the debt is redeemed, even if the default has been remedied.[148] In *Jumani v Mortgage Express* it was held that "*there was no obligation on [the lender's] part to terminate the receivership and/or cause the relevant properties to be returned to [the borrower] even if all the arrears were cleared, it being open to [the lender] to leave it to the Receivers to proceed to realise [the lender's] security.*"[149] Once receivers are appointed, the only unilateral action that the borrower can take to prevent the receivership from continuing, is to redeem the secured debt plus any costs and interest (including the receivers costs) pursuant to the terms of the mortgage.

148 *Jumani v Mortgage Express* [2013] EWHC 1571 (Ch)

149 *Jumani v Mortgage Express* [2013] EWHC 1571 (Ch) at paragraph 88

Third Parties

7.19. Occupiers or tenants contacted by receivers should follow the principles outlined above. In practical terms, there may be merit in contacting the borrower to ascertain the borrower's stance regarding the purported appointment and consider any action the borrower may be taking or whether there are merits in taking independent action.

Litigation brought by receivers

7.20. There is authority which supports the proposition that receivers can conduct litigation where they consider it necessary to allow them to discharge their duties or to exercise any of their powers.

7.21. In *Wheeler (M) & Co Ltd v Warren* it was held that a receiver "*must have power to get in the property in the only way possible – namely, by bringing an action in the name of the company*" even if the power to bring proceedings is not expressly granted by the mortgage.[150] Relying on *Wheeler, McDonald v McDonal* [2014] goes a little further:

> *The mortgage conditions have to be interpreted purposively: the clear purpose of the mortgage conditions was to enable the receivers to proceed to realise the charged property in an orderly and efficient way. The powers conferred on the receivers must therefore include power to do anything which is necessarily incidental to the exercise of the specified powers*[151]

150 Wheeler (M) & Co Ltd v Warren [1928] Ch 840

151 McDonald v McDonald [2015] 2 WLR 567

7.22. Receivers appointed under a fixed legal charge will need to check the conditions set out in the mortgage conditions and the appointment document to ascertain what (if any) express powers they have to conduct litigation and whether they are empowered to act as agent for the mortgagee, and/or agent for the lender or whether they must act in their own right.

7.23. Some mortgage conditions will expressly permit the receivers to act as agent for the mortgagor in bringing proceedings. Some mortgage conditions will also allow the receivers to act as agent for the mortgagee, or exercise the powers of the mortgagee, by way of proceedings. However, it is not uncommon for mortgage conditions to be silent as to express powers to pursue litigation, in which case the authorities noted at above may be relied upon.

Against third parties

7.24. Aside from acting as agents of the mortgagor, receivers may also act in litigation as donees of a power, as agent for the lender or in their own right.

7.25. Mortgage conditions or the appointment document, may grant the receivers the ability to exercise the powers granted to the lender. If exercising these powers, the receivers will do so as donee or as agent of the lender. In practice, this is sometimes encountered in possession claims where the receivers may be unable to determine interests of an occupier which bind the receivers. But the lender may have a clearer right to seek possession free from the interests of the occupier (e.g. an unauthorised tenant) and the receivers are granted the ability to exercise the rights of the lender. If receivers are granted the power to exercise the rights of the lender they will do so either as donee of the lender's power if the power is granted in the mortgage conditions, or as agent of the lender if the power is granted separately to the receivers in the appointment document a separate instrument.

7.26. The final category of cases is where receivers bring a claim in their own right. Examples where this may be appropriate are where the receivers require court directions (see paragraph 7.72 below) or where they have a claim in their own right which does not arise out of their receiver powers.

7.27. The receivers will also need to bring claims in their own name where the agency relationship between receivers and borrowers have come to an end, for example, where the borrower is deceased or insolvent.[152]

7.28. The decision on whether to issue proceedings, of whatever nature, is a serious one and receivers should take professional advice on whether they have the power to issue proceedings and, if so, in what capacity (as agent for mortgage, lender or in their own right) and advice concerning the merits and risks of a claim.

7.29. Where the claim is brought by the receivers acting as agents for the borrower, the claimant to the litigation should be formulated as follows: "Mr John Smith acting by Clare Brown and Paul Gray (Joint Fixed Charge Receivers)". This is subject to some exceptions, such as where the borrower is deceased or insolvent.[153]

7.30. Where the claim is brought by receivers acting as agents for the lender, the claimant to the litigation should be the name of the lender.

---

152 See Chapter 3 regarding powers

153 See paragraph 2.15

7.31. Where the claim is brought by the receivers in their own right or donee of a power, the claimant should be the name of the receivers.

Income

7.32. Receivers appointed under the Law of Property Act 1925 have a statutory power to pursue litigation to recover income:

Section 109

(3) The receiver shall have power to demand and recover all the income of which he is appointed receiver, by action or under section 72(1) of the Tribunals, Courts and Enforcement Act 2007 (commercial rent arrears recovery) , or otherwise, in the name either of the mortgagor or of the mortgagee, to the full extent of the estate or interest which the mortgagor could dispose of, and to give effectual receipts accordingly for the same, and to exercise any powers which may have been delegated to him by the mortgagee pursuant to this Act.

7.33. Action is not defined but would include court action together with other enforcement or recovery options.

7.34. Section 109(3) provides an express power to act "*in the name of either the mortgagor or of the mortgagee*". Thus the receivers, appointed solely with statutory powers, can decide on whether to pursue recovery action acting as the agent of the mortgagor or as the agent of the mortgagee.

7.35. The most common approach, and the one which limits the exposure of the lender, is to take action as agent for the borrower.

Possession

7.36. Claims for possession of the secured property are one of the most common types of claim brought by receivers. Such claims are usually brought by the receivers acting as agents for the borrower and exercising the borrower's right to possession.

7.37. However, receivers may also be able to exercise the lender's power of possession if they are granted the power to do so as donees of the lender's power under the mortgage conditions or the appointment document or as agents for the lender.

7.38. Possession claims are considered in more depth in Chapter 5.

Injunctions

7.39. Receivers may wish to seek injunctive relief against third parties to restrain acts or damage. For example, injunctive relief against managing agents who may refuse to co-operate with, or recognise the office, of the receivers and interfere with the management of the secured property.

7.40. If a cross-undertaking in damages is required as a condition of obtaining injunctive relief, receivers must carefully consider the source of funds that could be used to satisfy any undertaking e.g. income from the mortgaged property. The source of funds for the undertaking in damages which depend on which power the receivers are exercising: if they act as claimants in their own right, they will need to be provided with the undertaking and, similarly, if they are acting as agent for the lender, then the lender should provide the undertaking. In the former situation, receivers may wish to seek a separate indemnity from the lender so as to protect them from adverse risk if their own undertaking is called upon.

7.41. In circumstances where borrowers, or other third parties, persistently make court application to prevent or restrain receivers from exercising their duties or selling the property, receivers may seek civil restraint orders under Practice Direction 3C of the Civil Procedure Rules.[154]

<u>Costs orders</u>

7.42. The costs associated with litigation or other legal action are covered by the receivers' indemnity out of receivership assets. This extends to adverse costs orders in legal proceedings – such orders will be against the borrower where the receivers are engaged in the litigation as agents for the borrower. Where this is the case, care should be taken to ensure any such orders are properly worded so as to name the borrower as the party required to pay the costs order, not the receivers personally.

7.43. Adverse costs orders can take several forms and the court has a wide discretion.[155] For example, the court may order that the costs incurred by the receivers are not to be added to the mortgage debt. This does not automatically mean that the costs are not indemnified by the lender under the terms of the receivers' remuneration agreement or indemnity with the lender and any such contractual documents should be carefully considered. Receivers should be advised on the adverse costs risks of any litigation.

---

[154] See also *Perkin & Anor v Hawkins & Anor* [2025] EWHC 3053 (KB) for guidance on when receivers may be able to obtain an extended civil restraint order

[155] See section 51 of the Senior Courts Act 1981

Termination of receivership and litigation

7.44. Complications and risks can arise if the receivers' appointment is terminated whilst the receivers are engaged in litigation.[156] This is particularly the case where receivers are pursuing litigation as agent for the borrower. On termination of their appointment, whether that is by way of redemption, termination by the lender or otherwise, the receivers' agency powers will come to an end.[157] Receivers, and their solicitors, will lose the ability to conduct the litigation so should take prompt steps to withdraw from or discontinue the claim.[158]

Litigation concerning the borrower

7.45. It is necessary to distinguish between claims brought by the receivers against the borrower where they are acting in their own right, as against claims brought by receivers against the borrower where the receivers are exercising receivership powers.

7.46. Common types of claims against borrowers include:

- claims for possession brought by receivers against the borrower where the borrower is in possession;[159] and

- claims for injunctive relief against the borrower, for example, to restrain the borrower from interfering in the

156 See Chapter 8 regarding termination

157 See Chapter 3 regarding agency powers

158 Although care should be taken to understand the adverse cost consequences of discontinuance under Part 38 of the Civil Procedure Rules 1998

159 See paragraph 5.33

receivership, granting licences or tenancies, collecting rent, seeking to influence or control managing agents or occupiers or employees.[160]

7.47. It is not uncommon for borrowers to be added to litigation brought by receivers against third parties, for example, occupiers of secured properties. Borrowers may wish to be represented in a possession claim brought by receivers to evict the borrower's tenants.

7.48. It is not unheard of for borrowers to seek to appear at hearings or engage in correspondence with the court or third parties alleging that they are the "claimant". There is, understandably, some confusion where receivers are bringing a claim for possession as agent of the borrower (with the borrower being named as the claimant acting by the receivers). Such actions are not procedurally correct and can cause delay and increased costs. The correct course of action is for borrowers to seek to participate in the proceedings in their own right.

7.49. Borrowers may apply to the court to be added as a party under Rule 19.4 of the Civil Procedure Rules or on occasion the court may add the borrower at the request of the third party or of the court's own volition.

7.50. Similarly, it is common for borrowers to become Part 20 Defendants if a third party such as an occupier pursues a counterclaim/Part 20 claim in response to possession proceedings brought by receivers.

7.51. Borrowers may seek to challenge the appointment of the receivers or their actions by way of litigation. There are many causes of action that may be open to borrowers and the common ones can include: claims for declaratory and/or

160 See paragraph 7.39

injunctive relief around the appointment of the receivers and the action they are taking e.g. to collect income or seek possession/sale of secured property. Borrowers may wish to compel the performance of contracts they have previously entered into prior to the commencement of the receivership e.g. contracts for sale of the secured property.

7.52. Attempts by borrowers to restrain receivers from selling a property are often futile and it is considered to be only in exceptional circumstances that a delay would be ordered.[161] A borrower may also apply to court for an order under section 91 of the Law of Property Act 1925, which gives the court a discretion to direct a sale of the secured property. This discretion may be exercised even if the receivers are already engaged in a sale, although it has been held that there must be "*exceptional circumstances*" for the court to interfere with the receivers' sale.[162] Note that a sale contract entered into by receivers does not prevent the borrower from exercising its equity of redemption and paying off the mortgage debt, thereby frustrating the receivers' sale.[163]

7.53. It is also not uncommon for the lender to be involved in such litigation and to be named as a defendant. It is submitted that it is best practice, so as to manage the risk of potential conflicts of interest, for the lender and the receivers to have separate

---

161 See *Weldon (an executor of the will of J R Weldon, deceased) v Godiva Mortgages Ltd and others* [2024] EWHC 316 (KB) where the daughter of the deceased borrower was acting as executor of the borrower's will and the property was "*a beloved family home, which the [borrower] materially himself built*". See also *Lexham Securities Limited & Anor v Earlsfort Capital Partners Limited & Ors [2023] EWHC 909 (Ch)*

162 See *Fairmont Property Developers UK Ltd v Venus Bridging Ltd and others* [2025] EWCA Civ 1513

163 See *National Westminster Bank Plc v Hunter and Another* [2011] EWHC 3170 (Ch)

legal representatives. Separate representation also more effectively ensure separate decision making processes for the lender and the receivers, and may avoid allegations that the lender is directing or controlling the receivers.[164]

Litigation concerning the lender

7.54. It will be rare for receivers to issue proceedings against their appointing lender, given the nature of the relationship and the commercial realities. However, disputes can arise, particularly around the receivers' remuneration or obligations under indemnity provided by the lender to the receiver.

7.55. The extent of the obligations between the receivers and lender regarding remuneration and any indemnities will be governed by the wording of the mortgage conditions, the appointment document and any contractual indemnity (which may be a standalone document or it may form part of the appointment). Such documents must be carefully construed.

7.56. A lender may also seek to challenge the actions of receivers it has appointed if it considers that the receivers have breached their duties. Such cases are, however, rare.[165]

7.57. Lenders seeking to challenge requests or claims brought by receivers for remuneration or an indemnity will need to carefully construe the contractual documents – the mortgage conditions, the appointment document and any contractual indemnity.

---

164 See paragraph 3.83 regarding lender agency, direction and control

165 See *International Leisure Ltd and another v First National Trustee Company UK Ltd and others* [2012] EWHC 1971 (Ch) for an example of a case where a debenture holder sought to challenge the actions of a receiver

7.58. The common law regarding contractual indemnities will apply, such that losses caused by the receivers acting negligently, tortiously or beyond their powers will not be covered by any indemnity, unless the lender directed those acts.

7.59. Further, the receivers may be liable to the lender for losses caused to the lender by the receivers' negligence when they acted on their own. Claims under the Civil Liability (Contribution) Act 1978 can flow both ways between receivers and lender.

7.60. In practical terms, it is important for lenders to avoid interfering with, or providing directions to, the receivers in order to avoid inadvertently creating liability.

7.61. It is not uncommon for lenders to be joined as a party to litigation involving receivers and borrowers. Depending on the nature of the claim and risk of liability, it is sometimes convenient and cost effective for lenders and receivers to instruct the same lawyers where they have a substantially common interest. The risk of actual or potential conflicts of interest must be carefully managed and due to those risks, separate representation is usually preferable.

Litigation concerning third parties

7.62. There are many types of claim that third parties may seek to pursue against receivers. Examples include claims by contractual counterparties seeking damages and/or specific performance, claims by property occupiers/lessees/tenants, claims by landlords/lessors/freeholders or their agents (where the secured property is a leasehold interest) or claims brought by other charge holders.

7.63. It is necessary to carefully consider who the cause of action is against and whether the defendant to such claims should be the receivers in their personal capacity or claims where the defendant is actually the borrower.

7.64. The former type of claims include those where the receivers have personally contracted with third parties, or the receivers are personally accused of liability due to their own actions/inaction, for example, tortious behaviour or trespass.

7.65. Claims where the proper defendant and party liable is the borrower, rather than the receivers, include the following: claims where the borrower has breached contractual obligations or statutory obligations. This is the case even where the receivers' actions or proposed actions are said to cause the breach of contract or obligation, so long as the receivers are acting within their powers and bona fide.

7.66. Practical scenarios where these principles apply include the following:

7.67. Where the borrower entered into a contract with an agent to manage the secured property, collect rent and deal with tenants. If it is within the receivers' powers to do so, and they are acting bona fide and in good faith, they can terminate the contract or decline to perform the borrower's contractual obligations. Any claim for damages for breach of contract or specific performance will be against the borrower, and not against the receivers.

7.68. Where the borrower has breached repairing obligations / or statutory obligations to repair, any liability is generally on the borrower, not the receivers (unless the relevant legislation can be construed so as to convey liability onto the receivers).

7.69. Receivers should assert the powers and the limits of their liability, ideally in pre-action correspondence, so if litigation does ensue, the correct parties are identified, named and served. If this is not done properly by the claimant, receivers can seek to have claims against them struck out, or summary judgment entered in their favour, if they have been improperly sued and costs would follow the event in the usual way.

7.70. Third parties seeking to claim against receivers concerning contracts entered into by the borrower pre-dating the receivership, will have difficulty. Generally receivers acting as agents for the borrower are not obliged to perform the borrower's pre-existing contracts and the counterparty will be unable to sue the receivers for specific performance or damages.[166]

7.71. It has been held that firms who employ receivers are not vicariously liable for the acts and omissions of their employees who are appointed as receivers under the Law of Property Act 1925. The appointment is in a personal capacity and actions taken during the receivership appointment are not considered to be in the course of their employment.[167]

Other claims

Application for directions

7.72. Receivers may bring a claim in their own right. Examples where this may be appropriate are where the receivers require court directions; this may be appropriate where the receivers

---

166 See *Lathia v Dronsfield Bros Ltd* [1987] BCLC 321 and *Airlines Airspares Ltd v Handley Page Ltd* [1970] 2 WLR 163

167 *Yerbury v Azets Holdings Ltd* [2025] EWHC 757 (KB)

require court directions under section 35 of the Insolvency Act 1986 which states:

35 Application to court for directions

(1) A receiver or manager of the property of a company appointed under powers contained in an instrument, or the persons by whom or on whose behalf a receiver or manager has been so appointed, may apply to the court for directions in relation to any particular matter arising in connection with the performance of the functions of the receiver or manager.

(2) On such an application, the court may give such directions, or may make such order declaring the rights of persons before the court or otherwise, as it thinks just.

7.73. Application should be made in accordance with the requirements of The Insolvency (England and Wales) Rules 2016.

7.74. Applications for directions brought by receivers appointed over assets owned by individual rather than company borrowers, should be by way of a claim under Part 8 of the Civil Procedure Rules 1998 for declaratory relief.

Summary

7.75. It is common for receivers to be involved in litigation in the course of a receivership. Receivers may need to seek a court order in various circumstances, such as where they require a possession order to take possession of the property, whether they require injunctive relief to prevent interference by third parties in their actions or claims under contractual indemnities or for directions.

7.76. It is important to properly consider who the parties to the claim should be and, with regard to the receivers, in which capacity they are acting. For example, acting as agent for the borrower, or in their own right, or as agent for the lender.

7.77. Lenders may be involved in litigation, commonly claims brought by borrowers in relation to redemption or the receivers' appointment.

CHAPTER EIGHT

ENDING THE RECEIVERSHIP

8. Introduction

8.1. Receivership can come to an end via several means including redemption of the mortgage debt, termination of the appointment by the lender, acceptance of a resignation by the receivers, or on the death of a receiver.

8.2. There may be practical difficulties encountered when receivers retire or replacement receivers need to be appointed.

8.3. After termination has taken place, there are a range of post-termination duties and tasks that receivers must attend to in order to bring the receivership to a diligent conclusion.

Methods of termination

8.4. There are several ways in which the receivership can come to an end.

8.5. Where the secured debt is redeemed, the receivership is completed. Redemption may take place by way of sale of the mortgage property, refinance by the borrower or otherwise. When redemption occurs, the receivership comes to a natural conclusion and the receivers can no longer exercise any of their rights or powers. Simply showing evidence that the borrower will shortly be able to redeem is not enough to restrict the receivers' powers.[168]

8.6. The lender may terminate the appointment of the receivers at any time. Section 109(5) of the Law of Property Act 1925 provides:

(5) The receiver may be removed, and a new receiver may be appointed, from time to time by the mortgagee by writing under his hand.

8.7. The termination must be in writing. The wording "*under his hand*" is not defined in the Law of Property Act 1925 but it is suggested that a signed notice or letter of termination will be sufficient, absent any specific requirements in the mortgage conditions.[169] The lender may decide to terminate the receivership if, for example, it has come to terms with the borrower

8.8. It may be possible for receivers to unilateral resign their appointment. There is no statutory power for receivers to resign of their own volition or obligation on the lender to accept the resignation. Receivers may be entitled to resign if they are granted the power to do so under the appointment document, although this would be unusual. In practical terms, there is usually discussion and agreement between the lender and the receivers as to termination or the "standing down" of the receivers.

---

168 See *Gomba Holdings UK Ltd and others v Homan and another* [1986] 3 All ER 94, which also provides authority to indicate that the "*valid tender of the redemption price*" may be sufficient

169 It is common in practice for electronic signatures to be used

8.9. It is suggested that, if receivers wish to end their appointment but the resignation is not accepted by the lender, the receivers may apply to court for directions or declaratory relief.[170]

8.10. Practical difficulties can arise where one joint receiver may resign or retire from the employment or office of the firm that employs the receivers. The end of the employment or any director role as between the individual receiver and his employer/firm will not bring an end to his office as receiver. The receiver's appointment as a receiver is separate to any employment of company office that he or she may hold. Such changes in personnel, by way of resignation/retirement or otherwise, and the appointment of a replacement receiver to a joint receivership, should all be recorded formally in writing and in advance of such changes taking effect. Any appointment of a replacement receiver in a joint receivership, should be given by the lender in writing in the same manner in which the original appointment was made.

8.11. If a receiver dies whilst in office, the appointment is terminated, although if a replacement receiver is appointed quickly so as to maintain continuity, then the receivership will continue.[171] In the case of a sole receiver appointment, this occurs automatically on death. In the case of the death of one joint receiver, the receivership will continue with the sole surviving receiver until a replacement is appointed by the lender or the sole survivor appointment is terminated and then a re-appointment made with a new joint receiver.

---

170 See Chapter 7 regarding litigation and applications to court

171 *White's Mortgage, Re, Public Trustee v White.* [1943] Ch. 166 where a sole receiver died and was not replaced for fourteen months, which was held to be a "new transaction" and not merely a continuation

8.12. Receivers appointed by a second ranking mortgagee can be displaced by the later appointment of receivers by a prior ranking mortgagee. The first ranking mortgagee retains the power to "*come in and displace*" a receiver appointed by a second ranking mortgagee.[172]

8.13. If the charge under which receivers are appointed is set aside, or voidable, then the receivership will end automatically.

Lender considerations

8.14. There are various instances in which the lender may wish to bring the receivership to an end before it has reached its natural conclusion. For example, the lender may have come to terms with the borrower and be willing to allow the mortgagee/mortgagor relationship to continue.

8.15. A lender may lose confidence in the actions that the receivers are undertaking and may decide to pursue other enforcement options.

8.16. A lender may also wish to continue the receivership but appoint alternative receivers. There is a choice here to either terminate the appointment of the existing receivers and promptly appoint replacement receivers, in which case the receivership will be seen as continuous. The period of what is prompt is not clear and it is recommended to keep the interregnum as short as possible, for practical as well as legal reasons.[173]

---

172 See *Metropolitan Amalgamated Estates Ltd, Re, Fairweather v Metropolitan Amalgamated Estates Ltd* [1912] 2 Ch 497

173 In *White's Mortgage, Re, Public Trustee v White* [1943] Ch. 166 a period of fourteen months between the death of a sole receiver and the

8.17. The alternative option is to terminate the existing receivership and then make a new appointment, providing the usual pre-conditions are met. This would be recommended where the interregnum period will be material, although much depends on the facts of the case.

8.18. Before taking steps to terminate a receiver appointment, lenders should provide advance notice to the receivers of their intention to terminate or the likelihood of an imminent redemption. This is to allow the receivers time to deal with necessary steps to prepare for the termination.[174] Note that receivers involved in active litigation will face particular risks and difficulties if their appointment is terminated prior to the litigation being brought to an end.[175]

Post-Termination

8.19. There are various tasks that receivers must undertake immediately following the cessation of their appointment.

8.20. Where the borrower is a company, notice must be given to Companies House in accordance with section 859k of the Companies Act 2006 which states:

(3) Where a person appointed receiver or manager of a company's property or undertaking under powers contained in an instrument ceases to act as such a receiver or manager, the person must, on so ceasing—

---

appointment of a replacement was seen as too long a gap for the receivership to be continuous, rather it was seen as a new transaction

174 See paragraphs 8.19 to 8.24 regarding administrative steps following termination

175 See Chapter 7 regarding litigation

(a) give notice to the registrar of that fact, and

(b) give the registrar a notice containing—

(i) in the case of a charge created before 6th April 2013, the information specified in subsection (4), or

(ii) in the case of a charge created on or after 6th April 2013, the unique reference code allocated to the charge.

(4) The information referred to in subsections (2)(b)(i) and (3)(b)(i) is—

(a) the date of the creation of the charge;

(b) a description of the instrument (if any) creating or evidencing the charge;

(c) short particulars of the property or undertaking charged.

8.21. No time limit is specified but the inclusion of the words "*on so ceasing*" indicate that notice should be provided immediately. Failure to comply with these requirements is an offence.[176]

8.22. Receivers are also required to file accounts with Companies House in accordance with section 38 of the Insolvency Act 1986 which states as follows:

(2) The accounts shall be delivered within one month (or such longer period as the registrar may allow) after the expiration of 12 months from the date of his appointment and of every subsequent

[176] See section 859k (6)-(7) of the Companies Act 2006. The relevant form is RM02 available at https://assets.publishing.service.gov.uk/media/5a7c786640f0b62aff6c1e50/RM02_notice_of_ceasing_to_act_as_an_administrative_receiver_receiver_or_manager.pdf

period of 6 months, and also within one month after he ceases to act as receiver or manager.

(3) The requisite accounts shall be an abstract in the prescribed form showing—

(a) receipts and payments during the relevant period of 12 or 6 months, or

(c) where the receiver or manager ceases to act, receipts and payments during the period from the end of the period of 12 or 6 months to which the last preceding abstract related (or, if no preceding abstract has been delivered under this section, from the date of his appointment) up to the date of his so ceasing, and the aggregate amount of receipts and payments during all preceding periods since his appointment.

8.23. There are no such requirements where receivers are appointed over assets of individual borrowers. However, receivers are advised in all cases to prepare final accounts and appropriately deal with other administrative tasks, such as paying invoices, cancelling insurance and other contracts, notifying interested parties, updating Land Registry records if needed.[177]

8.24. The receivers should ensure they are remunerated in accordance with the terms of the engagement with the lender.[178] If the receivers are concerned that such sums may not be paid, or if they have agreed to delay receipt of remuneration until the secured property is sold at some future date, then the receivers can register a Form T restriction against the lender's charge on the title to the secured property

177 See paragraph 2.65 regarding notification to HM Land Registry

178 See paragraph 2.76 regarding remuneration

at HM Land Registry pursuant to section 42(1)(a) of the Land Registration Act 2002.[179]

Summary

8.25. There are various methods by which a receivership can come to an end: redemption and termination being the most common.

8.26. If receivers wish to seek the termination of their appointment, they are best advised to agree the resignation or termination with the lender or apply to court for declaratory relief if this cannot be agreed.

8.27. There may be circumstances where a lender needs to appoint a replacement receiver, following the resignation or death of an existing receiver and care must be taken as to whether the receivership is to continue, or in effect be a fresh appointment.

8.28. After termination, receivers will need to attend to a number of post-termination tasks regarding notification to relevant third parties, settling accounts and liabilities and cancelling any contracts that they have entered into. Finally, receivers will need to ensure any outstanding issues concerning their remuneration are settled.

179 See HM Land Registry Practice Guide 19: notices, restrictions and the protection of third-party interests in the register available at: https://www.gov.uk/government/publications/notices-restrictions-and-the-protection-of-third-party-interests-in-the-register/practice-guide-19-notices-restrictions-and-the-protection-of-third-party-interests-in-the-register#form-t

MORE BOOKS BY LAW BRIEF PUBLISHING

'The Electronic Communications Code: A Practical Guide – Second Edition' by Kerry Bretherton KC, James Castle, Mark Loveday
'A Practical Guide to the Independent School Standards – September 2023 Edition' by Sarah McKimm
'A Practical Guide to Estate Administration and Crypto Assets' by Richard Marshall
'A Practical Guide to Parental Alienation in Private and Public Law Children Cases' by Sam King QC & Frankie Shama
'Contested Heritage – Removing Art from Land and Historic Buildings' by Richard Harwood QC, Catherine Dobson, David Sawtell
'The Limits of Separate Legal Personality: When Those Running a Company Can Be Held Personally Liable for Losses Caused to Third Parties Outside of the Company' by Dr Mike Wilkinson
'A Practical Guide to Transgender Law' by Robin Moira White & Nicola Newbegin
'A Practical Guide to 'Stranded Spouses' in Family Law' by Mani Singh Basi
'A Practical Guide to Residential Freehold Conveyancing' by Lorraine Richardson
'A Practical Guide to Pensions on Divorce for Lawyers' by Bryan Scant
'A Practical Guide to Challenging Sham Marriage Allegations in Immigration Law' by Priya Solanki
'A Practical Guide to Digital Communications Evidence in Criminal Law' by Sam Willis
'A Practical Guide to Legal Rights in Scotland' by Sarah-Jane Macdonald
'A Practical Guide to New Build Conveyancing' by Paul Sams & Rebecca East
'A Practical Guide to Inherited Wealth on Divorce' by Hayley Trim
'A Practical Guide to Practice Direction 12J and Domestic Abuse in Private Law Children Proceedings' by Rebecca Cross & Malvika Jaganmohan
'A Practical Guide to Confiscation and Restraint' by Narita Bahra QC, John Carl Townsend, David Winch
'A Practical Guide to the Law of Forests in Scotland' by Philip Buchan
'A Practical Guide to Health and Medical Cases in Immigration Law' by Rebecca Chapman & Miranda Butler
'A Practical Guide to Bad Character Evidence for Criminal Practitioners by Aparna Rao
'A Practical Guide to Extradition Law post-Brexit' by Myles Grandison et al
'A Practical Guide to Hoarding and Mental Health for Housing Lawyers' by Rachel Coyle

'Stephens on Contractual Indemnities' by Richard Stephens
'A Practical Guide to the EU Succession Regulation' by Richard Frimston
'A Practical Guide to Solicitor and Client Costs – Second Edition' by Robin Dunne
'Constructive Dismissal – Practice Pointers and Principles' by Benjimin Burgher
'A Practical Guide to Religion and Belief Discrimination Claims in the Workplace' by Kashif Ali
'A Practical Guide to the Law of Medical Treatment Decisions' by Ben Troke
'Fundamental Dishonesty and QOCS in Personal Injury Proceedings: Law and Practice' by Jake Rowley
'A Practical Guide to the Law in Relation to School Exclusions' by Charlotte Hadfield & Alice de Coverley
'A Practical Guide to Divorce for the Silver Separators' by Karin Walker
'The Right to be Forgotten – The Law and Practical Issues' by Melissa Stock
'A Practical Guide to Planning Law and Rights of Way in National Parks, the Broads and AONBs' by James Maurici QC, James Neill et al
'A Practical Guide to Election Law' by Tom Tabori
'A Practical Guide to the Law in Relation to Surrogacy' by Andrew Powell
'A Practical Guide to Claims Arising from Fatal Accidents – Second Edition' by James Patience
'A Practical Guide to Asbestos Claims' by Jonathan Owen & Gareth McAloon
'A Practical Guide to Stamp Duty Land Tax in England and Northern Ireland' by Suzanne O'Hara
'A Practical Guide to the Law of Farming Partnerships' by Philip Whitcomb
'A Practical Guide to the Law of Unlawful Eviction and Harassment – Second Edition' by Stephanie Lovegrove
'A Practical Guide to Costs in Personal Injury Claims – Second Edition' by Matthew Hoe
'A Practical Guide to the General Data Protection Regulation (GDPR) – Second Edition' by Keith Markham
'A Practical Guide to Working with Litigants in Person and McKenzie Friends in Family Cases' by Stuart Barlow
'Protecting Unregistered Brands: A Practical Guide to the Law of Passing Off' by Lorna Brazell
'A Practical Guide to Secondary Liability and Joint Enterprise Post-Jogee' by Joanne Cecil & James Mehigan

'A Practical Guide to the Pre-Action RTA Claims Protocol for Personal Injury Lawyers' by Antonia Ford
'A Practical Guide to Neighbour Disputes and the Law' by Alexander Walsh
'A Practical Guide to Coercive Control for Legal Practitioners and Victims' by Rachel Horman
'A Practical Guide to the Law of Driverless Cars – Second Edition'
by Alex Glassbrook, Emma Northey & Scarlett Milligan
'A Practical Guide to TOLATA Claims' by Greg Williams
'A Practical Guide to Elderly Law – Second Edition' by Justin Patten
'A Practical Guide to Responding to Housing Disrepair and Unfitness Claims' by Iain Wightwick
'A Practical Guide to the Law of Bullying and Harassment in the Workplace' by Philip Hyland
'How to Be a Freelance Solicitor: A Practical Guide to the SRA-Regulated Freelance Solicitor Model' by Paul Bennett
'A Practical Guide to Prison Injury Claims' by Malcolm Johnson
'A Practical Guide to Advising Clients at the Police Station' by Colin Stephen McKeown-Beaumont
'A Practical Guide to Antisocial Behaviour Injunctions – Second Edition' by Iain Wightwick
'Practical Mediation: A Guide for Mediators, Advocates, Advisers, Lawyers, and Students in Civil, Commercial, Business, Property, Workplace, and Employment Cases' by Jonathan Dingle with John Sephton
'The Mini-Pupillage Workbook' by David Boyle
'A Practical Guide to Crofting Law' by Brian Inkster
'A Practical Guide to the Law of Domain Names and Cybersquatting' by Andrew Clemson
'A Practical Guide to the Law of Gender Pay Gap Reporting' by Harini Iyengar
'NHS Whistleblowing and the Law' by Joseph England
'Employment Law and the Gig Economy' by Nigel Mackay & Annie Powell
'A Practical Guide to Noise Induced Hearing Loss (NIHL) Claims' by Andrew Mckie, Ian Skeate, Gareth McAloon
'An Introduction to Beauty Negligence Claims – A Practical Guide for the Personal Injury Practitioner' by Greg Almond
'Intercompany Agreements for Transfer Pricing Compliance' by Paul Sutton
'Zen and the Art of Mediation' by Martin Plowman
'A Practical Guide to Adoption for Family Lawyers' by Graham Pegg